Chapter Tutorials
with Answer Key

(HOLT)

World History
The Human Journey

HOLT, RINEHART AND WINSTON

A Harcourt Education Company

Austin • Orlando • Chicago • New York • Toronto • London • San Diego

CUR
41
HRW
9-12
2005
CT

Cover description: John Glenn
Cover credit: NASA

Printed in the United States of America

ISBN 0-03-065737-7

8 9 10 11 054 09 08 07 06

Contents

Chapter Tutorials

TO THE TEACHER

Each chapter and unit of *World History: The Human Journey* has a corresponding chapter tutorial to provide a tool for other individuals, beside the teacher, who may be taking part in helping students learn. The tutorials provide parents, mentors, and peers the ability to work with students to cover key chapter material for future assessment.

CHAPTER 1

Chapter Tutorial

The Emergence of Civilization

IDENTIFYING TERMS Choose the term or name that correctly matches each definition.

_____ **1.** culture with three characteristics   **a.** nomads

_____ **2.** the study of human remains   **b.** pre-history

_____ **3.** wanderers   **c.** a civilization

_____ **4.** period before writing   **d.** hominids

_____ **5.** human/pre-human creatures   **e.** anthropology

UNDERSTANDING MAIN IDEAS

1. What methods do anthropologists and archaeologists use to explain pre-history?

_____

_____

2. What were some of the important characteristics of Cro-Magnon people?

_____

_____

3. What effect did the Neolithic agricultural revolution have on the lives of people living at that time?

_____

_____

4. What are the three major characteristics of a civilization?

_____

_____

5. What are the other two characteristics that usually mark a civilization?

_____

_____

Chapter 1 Tutorial, continued

REVIEWING THEMES

1. Economics How did improved farming methods lead to the development of civilizations?

_____

_____

2. Geography What similarities in physical environment did the first civilizations share?

_____

_____

3. Culture What characteristics of early *Homo sapiens* most set them apart from earlier hominids?

_____

_____

THINKING CRITICALLY

Finding the Main Idea Explain the economic, social, and geographic factors that led to the first civilizations.

_____

_____

_____

WRITING ABOUT HISTORY

Persuading Imagine you are an archaeologist. Write a description of the artifacts you might find in an excavation of an early civilization, and what their use might have been.

_____

_____

_____

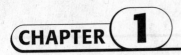
IDENTIFYING TERMS Choose the term or name that correctly matches each definition.

c (p. 11) **1.** culture with three characteristics   **a.** nomads

e (p. 6) **2.** the study of human remains   **b.** pre-history

a (p. 9) **3.** wanderers   **c.** a civilization

b (p. 4) **4.** period before writing   **d.** hominids

d (p. 6) **5.** human/pre-human creatures   **e.** anthropology

UNDERSTANDING MAIN IDEAS

1. What methods do anthropologists and archaeologists use to explain pre-history?

Archaeologists dig into ancient settlements and study the artifacts. Anthropologists study the human remains. (p. 6)

2. What were some of the important characteristics of Cro-Magnon people?

They made better tools than Neanderthals, and were artists and effective hunters. (p. 8)

3. What effect did the Neolithic agricultural revolution have on the lives of people living at that time?

It allowed the people to settle into towns instead of being nomads. (p. 10)

4. What are the three major characteristics of a civilization?

The ability to create a food surplus, to establish towns or cities with some form of government, and to allow the population to specialize in their areas of work. (p. 11)

5. What are the other two characteristics that usually mark a civilization?

The creation of a calendar and the development of some form of writing. (p. 13)

REVIEWING THEMES

1. Economics How did improved farming methods lead to the development of civilizations?

People could trade food for products, and so diversified work groups developed. These included artisans, laborers, merchants, and traders who not only transported goods to be sold but also passed along ideas to different groups. This led to cultural diffusion. (p. 12)

2. Geography What similarities in physical environment did the first civilizations share?

A hot climate and flooding. (p. 11)

3. **Culture** What characteristics of early *Homo sapiens* most set them apart from earlier hominids?

They wore animal skins, used fire for warmth and cooking, buried their dead, and used tools. (p. 8)

THINKING CRITICALLY

Finding the Main Idea Explain the economic, social, and geographic factors that led to the first civilizations.

Climate and flooding in river valleys produced a rich soil that enabled farmers to produce a food surplus. Populations then increased with better food, and the villages became cities. (p. 12)

WRITING ABOUT HISTORY

Persuading Imagine you are an archaeologist. Write a description of the artifacts you might find in an excavation of an early civilization, and what their use might have been.

Answers will vary.

STUDY TIPS

1. Have students make flash cards of the important terms and people listed at the beginning of each section. Students can work in pairs to test each other on the information.

2. Ask students the Read to Discover questions listed at the beginning of each section. If the students have trouble answering them, help them find corresponding portions of the text and reread them.

Chapter Tutorial

The First Civilizations

IDENTIFYING TERMS

_____ **1.** a form of writing

_____ **2.** money as a measure of value

_____ **3.** family of rulers

_____ **4.** Persian prophet

_____ **5.** belief in one God

a. Zoroaster

b. dynasty

c. monotheism

d. hieroglyphics

e. money economy

UNDERSTANDING MAIN IDEAS

1. What evidence indicates that Egyptians were creating a civilization?

_____

_____

2. What benefits did strong Pharaohs bring to Egyptian kingdoms?

_____

_____

3. What accomplishments did the Egyptians make in science and math?

_____

_____

4. Why did the Phoenicians become traders?

_____

_____

5. How was society in Sumer different from society in Egypt?

_____

_____

Chapter 2 Tutorial, continued

REVIEWING THEMES

1. **Global Relations** How did trade promote cultural exchanges between ancient civilizations?

   _____

   _____

2. **Geography** What physical features of the Nile Valley contributed to the rise of civilization there?

   _____

   _____

3. **Culture** What did the Egyptians achieve in architecture and the arts?

   _____

   _____

THINKING CRITICALLY

1. **Evaluating** What aspects of the *Code of Hammurabi* laws are evident in our legal system today?

   _____

   _____

2. **Supporting a Point of View** Explain why Sumer was vunerable to invasions.

   _____

   _____

WRITING ABOUT HISTORY

Comparing Write a paragraph comparing the rights of women today to the rights that Egyptian women enjoyed.

_____

_____

_____

IDENTIFYING TERMS

_d (p. 22)_ **1.** a form of writing

a. Zoroaster

_e (p. 43)_ **2.** money as a measure of value

b. dynasty

_b (p. 22)_ **3.** family of rulers

c. monotheism

_a (p. 40)_ **4.** Persian prophet

d. hieroglyphics

_c (p. 25)_ **5.** belief in one God

e. money economy

UNDERSTANDING MAIN IDEAS

1. What evidence indicates that Egyptians were creating a civilization?

They were mining metals, developing writing, and farming. (p. 22)

2. What benefits did strong Pharaohs bring to Egyptian kingdoms?

They had absolute power, created strong armies, gained land, and held their empires together. (p. 24)

3. What accomplishments did the Egyptians make in science and math?

They created a number system and developed geometry. (p. 27)

4. Why did the Phoenicians become traders?

Phoenicia had little fertile land, and the Lebanon Mountains made migration to the east difficult. Thus, the Phoenicians turned to trading on the sea. (p. 41)

5. How was society in Sumer different from society in Egypt?

They did not believe in a rewarding afterlife, education was only for upperclass men, and women did not have the same status as men. (p. 34)

REVIEWING THEMES

1. Global Relations How did trade promote cultural exchanges between ancient civilizations?

Peoples often adopted aspects of cultures with which they came in contact. (p. 29)

2. Geography What physical features of the Nile Valley contributed to the rise of civilization there?

A sunny, frost-free climate and floods that fertilized the plains made it easy to grow crops. (p. 21)

3. Culture What did the Egyptians achieve in architecture and the arts?

The pyramids and sculpture (p. 27)

THINKING CRITICALLY

1. Evaluating What aspects of the *Code of Hammurabi* are evident in our legal system today?

Penalties for false testimony, death sentence for severe crimes, and liability for poor work-manship. (p. 36)

2. Supporting a Point of View Explain why Sumer was vunerable to invasions.

It was not geographically isolated, making invasions easy. (p. 31)

WRITING ABOUT HISTORY

Comparing Write a paragraph comparing the rights of women today to the rights that Egyptian women enjoyed.

Student answers will vary. Students may include ownership of property, writing their own wills, and equals of men socially and in business. (p. 28)

STUDY TIPS

1. Have students create a time line for the development of Egyptian arts, writing, architecture, math, and science.

2. Ask students to write a paragraph on how they might have experienced life as a Hebrew slave in Egypt.

Chapter Tutorial

Ancient Indian Civilization

IDENTIFYING TERMS

_____ 1. winds   **a.** polytheism

_____ 2. fortress   **b.** Sanskrit

_____ 3. a language   **c.** monsoon

_____ 4. belief in many Gods   **d.** polygyny

_____ 5. more than one wife   **e.** citadel

UNDERSTANDING MAIN IDEAS

1. How is a civilization's location near a waterway beneficial to development?

_____

_____

2. What was the impact of Indo-Aryan migration?

_____

_____

3. In what way did the "epics" help to spread religious understanding and ideals?

_____

_____

4. How did the Guptas expand their power?

_____

_____

5. Why was the Gupta rule known as a "golden age" in Indian history?

_____

_____

Chapter 3 Tutorial, continued

REVIEWING THEMES

1. Economics Explain the different ways in which the Indo-Aryans and Mauryans controlled the economy.

_____

_____

2. Geography How did the physical geography of India lead to the development of a civilization?

_____

_____

3. Culture What was the cultural impact of Aśoka's rule over most of India?

_____

_____

THINKING CRITICALLY

1. Finding the Main Idea What sources do scholars use to find out about daily life in ancient India?

_____

_____

2. Supporting a Point of View Indicate which cultural advances of ancient India you believe to be the most important and why.

_____

_____

WRITING ABOUT HISTORY

Persuading Write a paragraph describing the four main beliefs of Buddhism.

_____

_____

_____

_____

IDENTIFYING TERMS

_c (p. 52)_ **1.** winds   **a.** polytheism

_e (p. 53)_ **2.** fortress   **b.** Sanskrit

_b (p. 56)_ **3.** a language   **c.** monsoon

_a (p. 62)_ **4.** belief in many Gods   **d.** polygyny

_d (p. 69)_ **5.** more than one wife   **e.** citadel

UNDERSTANDING MAIN IDEAS

1. How is a civilization's location near a waterway beneficial to development?

The inhabitants are able to conduct trade by sea, expand their contacts, and travel abroad. (p. 52)

2. What was the impact of Indo-Aryan migration?

They brought with them a new social order and the Sanskrit language. They also contributed new religious ideas about the nature of the world. (p. 58)

3. In what way did the "epics" help spread religious understanding and ideals?

They could be heard and understood by people of all classes. (p. 60)

4. How did the Guptas expand their power?

By conquering more territory and intermarriage. (p. 68)

5. Why was the Gupta rule known as a "golden age" in Indian history?

Society prospered, great progress was made in the arts, and government was less centralized, giving more power to local leaders. (p. 68)

REVIEWING THEMES

1. Economics Explain the different ways in which the Indo-Aryan and Mauryans controlled the economy.

Indo-Aryan rajas controlled the land and drew wealth from the farmers who worked it. Mauryan rulers took one quarter of each harvest in taxes. (p. 69)

2. Geography How did the physical geography of India lead to the development of a civilization?

River valleys and fertile plains allowed easy farming and trade, while vast mountain ranges discouraged invasion. (p. 52)

3. Culture What was the cultural impact of Aśoka's rule over most of India?

Political advancement and peace for the nation (p. 67)

THINKING CRITICALLY

1. **Finding the Main Idea** What sources do scholars use to find out about daily life in ancient India?

   Archaeology, written material, and art (p. 50)

2. **Supporting a Point of View** Indicate which cultural advances of ancient India you believe to be the most important and why.

   Students may choose from education, math and astronomy, art, architecture, and medicine. (p. 71)

WRITING ABOUT HISTORY

Persuading Write a paragraph describing the four main beliefs of Buddhism.

Students should write about the "Four Noble Truths." (p. 64)

STUDY TIPS

1. Have students discuss the differences between Buddhism and Hinduism.

2. Have students write a paragraph comparing and contrasting ancient Indian medicine with modern medicine.

CHAPTER 4

Chapter Tutorial

Ancient Chinese Civilization

IDENTIFYING TERMS

_____ **1.** fertile yellow soil

_____ **2.** organized government

_____ **3.** tools for divination

_____ **4.** family record

_____ **5.** school of philosophy

a. bureaucracy

b. oracle bones

c. Legalism

d. loess

e. genealogy

UNDERSTANDING MAIN IDEAS

1. What problems and benefits did the Huang River bring to the Chinese people?

_____

_____

2. How is Chinese writing different from the writing of the West?

_____

_____

3. Why did the Zhou dynasty collapse?

_____

_____

4. What did the Legalists teach?

_____

_____

5. What did the ancient Chinese achieve in science and technology?

_____

_____

Chapter 4 Tutorial, continued

REVIEWING THEMES

1. **Economics** What was the Shang dynasty's economy primarily based on?

_____

_____

2. **Geography** What are the three rivers systems of China Proper?

_____

_____

3. **Culture** Why did Chinese culture develop in isolation?

_____

_____

THINKING CRITICALLY

1. **Finding the Main Idea** How did the idea of the Mandate of Heaven influence Chinese government?

_____

_____

2. **Supporting a Point of View** Explain the principal idea of yin and yang.

_____

_____

WRITING ABOUT HISTORY

Persuading Write a paragraph explaining the teachings and/or influence of Confucius.

_____

_____

_____

_____

_____

_____

IDENTIFYING TERMS

d (p. 78) **1.** fertile yellow soil   **a.** bureaucracy

a (p. 81) **2.** organized government   **b.** oracle bones

b (p. 82) **3.** tools for divination   **c.** Legalism

e (p. 93) **4.** family record   **d.** loess

c (p. 91) **5.** school of philosophy   **e.** genealogy

UNDERSTANDING MAIN IDEAS

1. What problems and benefits did the Huang River bring to the Chinese people?

Problems: flooding
Benefits: fertile soil (pp. 76–79)

2. How is Chinese writing different from the writing of the West?

Chinese writing consists of ideographs instead of letters. (pp. 80–83)

3. Why did the Zhou dynasty collapse?

Local leaders fought among themselves and were attacked by outsiders. (pp. 84–88)

4. What did the Legalists teach?

Power without virtue and harsh laws (pp. 91–92)

5. What did the ancient Chinese achieve in science and technology?

They proved the year was slightly longer than 365 days through advanced astronomy.
They also invented the seismograph, the sundial, paper, and acupuncture. (p. 95)

REVIEWING THEMES

1. Economics What was the Shang dynasty's economy primarily based on?

Agriculture. (p. 81)

2. Geography What are the three rivers systems of China Proper?

The Huang, the Chang, and the Xi. (p. 76)

3. Culture Why did Chinese culture develop in isolation?

Great distances, rugged mountains, and harsh deserts separated the Chinese from other civilizations. (p. 79)

THINKING CRITICALLY

1. Finding the Main Idea How did the idea of the Mandate of Heaven influence Chinese government?

Each new ruler of a territory during the Zhou dynasty had to renew or swear a pledge of loyalty to the God of Heaven. The Zhou rulers felt this pledge would keep the territorial rulers loyal. The Mandate of Heaven was also used to depose dynasties. Those who wished to take over the existing dynasty would assert that its leaders were unfit to rule because they had lost the Mandate of Heaven. (p. 84)

2. Supporting a Point of View Explain the principal idea of yin and yang and give an example.

The principal idea is that everything in the world results from a balance between two forces, yin/female and yang/male. Students may offer another example, such as light and dark. (p. 89)

WRITING ABOUT HISTORY

Persuading Write a paragraph explaining the teachings and\or influence of Confucius.

Students may write about the three concepts of Confucius: importance of family, respect for elders, and reverence for ancestors. Responses will vary. (p. 90)

STUDY TIPS

1. Have students create a time line of Chinese dynasties.

2. Ask students to draw a diagram illustrating the main concepts of Buddism, Confucianism, and Daoisim. Ask them to describe how each might have influenced the development of Chinese civilization.

Chapter Tutorial

The Greek City States

IDENTIFYING TERMS

_____ **1.** painting on plaster

_____ **2.** privileged social class

_____ **3.** government run by citizens

_____ **4.** bring in

_____ **5.** send out

a. democracy

b. fresco

c. import

d. aristocracy

e. export

UNDERSTANDING MAIN IDEAS

1. Why was the polis such an important part of Greek life?

_____

_____

2. What kind of information did Homer provide in the *Iliad* and the *Odyssey*?

_____

_____

3. What conditions or developments helped promote the rise of democracy in Athens?

_____

_____

4. What were the main activities for people in Athens?

_____

_____

5. What happened in Greece after the Peloponnesian War?

_____

_____

_____

Chapter 5 Tutorial, continued

REVIEWING THEMES

1. **Economics** How did the introduction of money in Athens in 600 B.C. stimulate trade?

_____

_____

2. **Geography** How did the geography of Greece affect the way its early civilizations grew?

_____

_____

3. **Culture** Who was permitted to be a citizen and participate in politics in Athens?

_____

_____

THINKING CRITICALLY

1. **Finding the Main Idea** What were the outcomes of the Persian Wars and Peloponnesian War?

_____

_____

2. **Supporting a Point of View** Compare the social classes in Spartan society with those in Athenian society.

_____

_____

WRITING ABOUT HISTORY

Persuading Write a brief paragraph describing life from an Athenian woman's point of view.

_____

_____

_____

IDENTIFYING TERMS

b (p.107) **1.** painting on plaster   **a.** democracy

d (p.111) **2.** privileged social class   **b.** fresco

a (p.112) **3.** government run by citizens   **c.** import

c (p.118) **4.** bring in   **d.** aristocracy

e (p.118) **5.** send out   **e.** export

UNDERSTANDING MAIN IDEAS

1. Why was the polis such an important part of Greek life?

Everything the people needed was within the polis. (pp. 106–109)

2. What kind of information did Homer provide in the *Iliad* and the *Odyssey*?

The Iliad *tells the story of the Trojan War. The* Odyssey *tells the story of Odysseus's journey home from the war. (pp. 110–112)*

3. What conditions or developments helped promote the rise of democracy in Athens?

Cleisthenes made Athens a direct democracy. Solon allowed more citizens to hold office. (pp. 113–117)

4. What were the main activities for people in Athens?

Men farmed, provided goods, engaged in trade, and participated in public life; women managed the household and raised children. Girls learned to manage households and boys attended school. (pp. 118–120)

5. What happened in Greece after the Peloponnesian Wars?

Greece was politically unstable. (p. 125)

REVIEWING THEMES

1. Economics How did the introduction of money in Athens in 600 B.C. stimulate trade?

It became easier to buy and sell goods. (p. 115)

2. Geography How did the geography of Greece affect the way its early civilizations grew?

Mountains isolated the earlier civilizations. Communication and travel were difficult. People focused on the sea and trading, which broadened foreign influence. (pp. 106–109)

3. **Culture** Who was permitted to be a citizen and participate in politics in Athens?

   Only free Athenian men. (p. 115)

THINKING CRITICALLY

1. **Finding the Main Idea** What were the outcomes of the Persian Wars and Peloponnesian War?

   Greece was politically unstable after the Persian Wars until the Delian League was formed, creating alliances between the states. (p. 123) However, after the Peloponnesian War, much of that stability was gone. Many in Greece thought that only a foreign power could bring stability to Greece again. (p. 125)

2. **Supporting a Point of View** Compare the social classes in Spartan society with those in Athenian society.

   Citizens in Athens and equals in Sparta were males who could vote and own property. Metics in Athens and half-citizens in Sparta were free and paid taxes but could not take part in government or own land. Athen's slaves and Sparta's helots had no political rights. (pp. 113–115)

WRITING ABOUT HISTORY

Persuading Write a brief paragraph describing life from an Athenian woman's point of view.

Answers will vary. Students may write about the home and family life of women in Athens. (p. 119)

STUDY TIPS

1. Have students explain why scholars know more about the government and society of Athens than they do about Sparta.

2. Ask students to draw a diagram that shows similarites and differences in the ideas and beliefs of Solon, Peisistratus, Cleithenes, and Pericles.

Chapter Tutorial

Greece's Golden and Hellenistic Ages

IDENTIFYING TERMS

_____ **1.** study of reality and existence   **a.** Pythagorean Theorem

_____ **2.** founder of medical science   **b.** phalanx

_____ **3.** rows of soldiers   **c.** philosophy

_____ **4.** 325–145 B.C.   **d.** Hellenistic Age

_____ **5.** mathematical theory   **e.** Hippocrates

UNDERSTANDING MAIN IDEAS

1. How did the Greeks of the golden age use art to express their values and ideals?

_____

_____

2. How did Greeks of the golden age comment on their society through literature, comedy, and drama?

_____

_____

3. What three empires were created from the conquests of Alexander the Great?

_____

_____

4. What effect did Hellenistic society have on women?

_____

_____

5. How did Eratosthenes calculate the distance around the Earth with such amazing accuracy?

_____

_____

_____

_____

Chapter 6 Tutorial, continued

REVIEWING THEMES

1. Economics Why was the Hellenistic Age a time of prosperity for so many?

_____

_____

2. Geography The power that finally united Greece came from north of the Greek Peninsula. Who led the armies that forced the Greek city-states into the new League of Corinth?

_____

_____

3. Culture What was the impact of philosophers on Greek culture?

_____

_____

THINKING CRITICALLY

1. Finding the Main Idea Why were the 400s B.C. generally known as the golden age of Greece?

_____

_____

2. Supporting a Point of View Provide evidence to support the claim that the approach to history used by Herodotus and Thucydides was a good system.

_____

_____

WRITING ABOUT HISTORY

Persuading Write a brief paragraph supporting the view that contact with outside cultures was a positive influence on Greece.

_____

_____

_____

_____

_____

Greece's Golden and Hellenistic Ages

IDENTIFYING TERMS

_c (p. 133)_ **1.** study of reality and existence   **a.** Pythagorean Theorem

_e (p. 135)_ **2.** founder of medical science   **b.** phalanx

_b (p. 138)_ **3.** rows of soldiers   **c.** philosophy

_d (p. 128)_ **4.** 325 B.C.–145 B.C.   **d.** Hellenistic Age

_a (p. 135)_ **5.** mathematical theory   **e.** Hippocrates

UNDERSTANDING MAIN IDEAS

1. How did the Greeks of the golden age use art to express their values and ideals?

They glorified humans; showed harmony, balance, and moderation in life; and combined beauty with usefulness. (pp. 130–132)

2. How did Greeks of the golden age comment on their society through literature, comedy, and drama?

Histories became more accurate, epic tales and dramas told of their struggles, and the main characters in comedies solved the Greeks' problems and gave hope to the audience. (pp. 134–137)

3. What three empires were created from the conquests of Alexander the Great?

It was divided into Macedon, Egypt, and Syria. (p. 141)

4. What effect did Hellenistic society have on women?

They appeared more in public and won new rights regarding property. (p. 142)

5. How did Eratosthenes calculate the distance around the Earth with such amazing accuracy?

By finding the angle of the sun's rays from different points on the globe. (p. 145)

REVIEWING THEMES

1. Economics Why was the Hellenistic Age a time of prosperity for so many?

The middle-ranked groups prospered from the spread of Greek culture. In addition, cities along trade routes became commercial centers and prospered. (p. 142)

2. Geography The power that finally united Greece came from north of the Greek Peninsula. Who led the armies that forced the city-states into the new League of Corinth?

Philip II, King of Macedonia (p. 138)

3. **Culture** What was the impact of philosphers on Greek culture?

   They introduced debate about ethics, wisdom, and high ideals and expanded the influence of scientific principles to everyday life. (p. 133–137)

THINKING CRITICALLY

1. **Finding the Main Idea** Why were the 400s B.C. generally known as the golden age of Greece?

   They signified Greece's entrance into a new era of cultural progress. (p. 130)

2. **Supporting a Point of View** Provide evidence to support the claim that the approach to history used by Herodotus and Thucydides was a good system.

   It resulted in a more accurate, honest, and fair view of events because their stories were told at the time they were happening. Herdodotus was always careful to make it clear how he was telling the story—either based on his personally witnessing the event, or based on secondhand information. (p. 136)

WRITING ABOUT HISTORY

Persuading Write a brief paragraph supporting the view that contact with outside cultures was a positive influence on Greece.

Students may write that cultural diversity was beneficial because it gave the Greeks a broader view of the world.

STUDY TIPS

1. Have students select a piece of Greek art and explain how it expresses the four basic Greek ideals.

2. Ask students to write letters to Hippocrates explaining why they admire his work.

Name _____ Class _____ Date _____

IDENTIFYING TERMS Choose the term or name that correctly matches each definition.

_____ **1.** powerful landowners   **a.** patricians

_____ **2.** farmers and workers   **b.** gladiator

_____ **3.** rule of three   **c.** plebians

_____ **4.** a trained fighter   **d.** Ovid

_____ **5.** famous poet   **e.** triumvirate

UNDERSTANDING MAIN IDEAS

1. How did the Conflict of the Orders change how the Roman Republic was governed?

_____

_____

2. What problems occurred as a result of Rome's expansion?

_____

_____

3. How might the history of the Roman Republic have been different if Caesar had shown less mercy?

_____

_____

4. In what areas did Rome make great contributions to the world? Give examples.

_____

_____

5. What were some of the causes of the decline of the Western Roman Empire?

_____

_____

Chapter 7 Tutorial, continued

REVIEWING THEMES

1. Economics What impact, if any, did slavery have on the Roman economy?

_____

_____

2. Geography Explain why geography both helped and hindered Rome's rise to power.

_____

_____

3. Culture What ideas and inventions did the Romans borrow from the Greeks?

_____

_____

THINKING CRITICALLY

1. Finding the Main Idea Contrast the daily life of Roman citizens and residents.

_____

_____

2. Supporting a Point of View Why did the Romans come to consider Christianity a threat?

_____

_____

WRITING ABOUT HISTORY

Persuading Write a paragraph explaining how Rome's relationship with the people it conquered changed over time.

_____

_____

_____

_____

_____

_____

IDENTIFYING TERMS Choose the term or name that correctly matches each definition.

_a (p. 153)_ **1.** powerful landowners   **a.** patricians

_c (p. 153)_ **2.** farmers and workers   **b.** gladiator

_e (p. 159)_ **3.** rule of three   **c.** plebians

_b (p. 165)_ **4.** a trained fighter   **d.** Ovid

_d (p. 167)_ **5.** famous poet   **e.** triumvirate

UNDERSTANDING MAIN IDEAS

1. How did the Conflict of the Orders change how the Roman Republic was governed?

Over time, plebians increased their power through demands and strikes, which resulted in a written code of law and weakened the distinction between patricians and plebians. (p. 153)

2. What problems occurred as a result of Rome's expansion?

Because Rome was now so vast and remained a republic, the Senate gained almost complete control over the army and foreign policy. Soldiers returning from war found their farms in ruins, and lacking the money to restore them, they went to the city for work but ended up depending on the government for food. (p. 157)

3. How might the history of the Roman Republic have been different if Caesar had shown less mercy?

He would not have been murdered and would have governed Rome much longer. (p. 159)

4. In what areas did Rome make great contributions to the world? Give examples.

Examples will vary but may include construction of roads that were left behind after the conquering Romans left; achievements in medicine, astronomy, geography, engineering, architecture, art, literature, and language. (pp. 163, 166–167)

5. What were some of the causes of the decline of the Western Roman Empire?

The Empire stopped expanding, civil unrest, barbarian invasions, and inflation. (p. 172–177)

REVIEWING THEMES

1. Economics What impact, if any, did slavery have on the Roman economy?

Historians do not believe that slavery was essential to the Roman economy. With so many poor workers available, the labor of a free worker would have been as cheap as or cheaper than slave labor. A person gained status as well as an easier lifestyle by owning slaves. (p. 164)

2. Geography Explain why geography both helped and hindered Rome's rise to power.

Rome's location between mountains and seas made Italy an excellent base from which to control both the eastern and western halves of the region. However, several mountain passageways, aside from offering relatively easy travel, also provided a route for invasion by enemy armies. (p. 150)

3. Culture What ideas and inventions did the Romans borrow from the Greeks?

The Romans used scientific knowledge from the Greeks to plan cities, build water and sewage systems, and improve farming and livestock breeding. (p. 166)

THINKING CRITICALLY

1. Finding the Main Idea Contrast the daily life of Roman citizens and residents.

Rich citizens usually had both a city and country home, running water and baths, and time for recreation and leisure. Most of Rome's residents lived in sparsely furnished, crowded apartments and could barely make a living. (p. 164)

2. Supporting a Point of View Why did the Romans come to consider Christianity a threat?

At first the Roman government viewed Christianity as a Jewish sect. Soon, however, the Christians began to speak out against the idea of worshiping the Emporer and tried to convert others to Christianity. The Romans saw this as an attack on Roman religion and law and soon outlawed Christianity because they feared an uprising. (p. 170)

WRITING ABOUT HISTORY

Persuading Write a paragraph explaining how Rome's relationship with the people it conquered changed over time.

Students may write about the way Rome allowed the peoples it conquered to remain mostly independent. (p. 154)

STUDY TIPS

1. Have students draw a time line detailing the fall of the Western Roman Empire.

2. Ask students the Read to Discover questions listed at the beginning of each section. If the students have trouble answering them, help them find corresponding portions of the text and reread them.

CHAPTER 8

Chapter Tutorial

Africa

IDENTIFYING TERMS Choose the term or name that correctly matches each definition.

_____ 1. those who study language

_____ 2. tales passed by being told

_____ 3. dry grasslands

_____ 4. lineage through the mother

_____ 5. unique African culture

a. oral tradition

b. matrilineal

c. linguists

d. savannas

e. Swahili

UNDERSTANDING MAIN IDEAS

1. How was early African society organized?

_____

_____

2. What was the relationship of the Kingdom of Kush to Egypt?

_____

_____

3. Why was the control of gold mining important in East Africa?

_____

_____

4. What unique culture developed in coastal East Africa, and what factors bound the different peoples of this culture together?

_____

_____

5. What role do scholars think women played in many African societies?

_____

_____

Chapter 8 Tutorial, continued

REVIEWING THEMES

1. Economics What types of goods were traded in Africa, and how did they meet people's needs?

_____

_____

2. Geography What geographical feature made trade and commerce difficult in many parts of Africa?

_____

_____

3. Global Relations How did the rulers of African kingdoms get what they wanted from others?

_____

_____

THINKING CRITICALLY

1. Finding the Main Idea What were the predominate patterns of life in many early African societies?

_____

_____

2. Supporting a Point of View How does the study of modern languages help us understand African history?

_____

_____

WRITING ABOUT HISTORY

Persuading Write a brief paragraph explaining how the people of Africa were able to build complex civilizations and share cultural ideas with each other and with people from other lands.

_____

_____

_____

IDENTIFYING TERMS Choose the term or name that correctly matches each definition.

_c (p. 184)_ **1.** those who study language

a. oral tradition

_a (p. 184)_ **2.** tales passed by being told

b. matrilineal

_d (p. 182)_ **3.** dry grasslands

c. linguists

_b (p. 186)_ **4.** lineage through the mother

d. savannas

_e (p. 191)_ **5.** unique African culture

e. Swahili

UNDERSTANDING MAIN IDEAS

1. How was early African society organized?

It was organized into matrilineal societies. (p. 186)

2. What was the relationship of the Kingdom of Kush to Egypt?

At first Kush engaged in trade and cultural exchanges with Egypt. In about 1520 B.C., Kush came under Egypt's control. About 710 B.C., Kush conquered Upper Egypt and ruled all of Egypt for 50 years. (pp. 187–189)

3. Why was the control of gold mining important in East Africa?

It led to power and wealth. (pp. 191–192)

4. What unique culture developed in coastal East Africa and what factors bound the different peoples of this culture together?

The Swahili culture developed in East Africa. The people of the culture spoke Swahili—a Bantu language with Arabic and Persian influences. Swahili speakers did not form one ethnic group but were bound together by language and trade. (p. 191)

5. What role do scholars think women played in many African societies?

They played a crucial role in social and economic life as primary farmers. (p. 186)

REVIEWING THEMES

1. Economics What types of goods were traded in Africa, and how did they meet people's needs?

Gold, ivory, hides, and tortoise shells were traded for goods people needed. (p. 191)

2. Geography What geographical feature made trade and commerce difficult in many parts of Africa?

The Sahara (p. 182)

3. **Global Relations** How did the rulers of African kingdoms get what they wanted from others?

By trade and conquest. (pp. 191–195)

THINKING CRITICALLY

1. **Finding the Main Idea** What were the predominate patterns of life in many early African societies?

Most Africans lived in small, independent farming, herding, or fishing villages; ties of kinship and age bound each society together. (p. 186)

2. **Supporting a Point of View** How does the study of modern languages help us understand African history?

By studying modern African languages, scientists can learn about the migrations of the early inhabitants of Africa. (p. 184)

WRITING ABOUT HISTORY

Persuading Write a brief paragraph explaining how the people of Africa were able to build complex civilizations and share cultural ideas with each other and with people from other lands.

Answers will vary. Students may answer that this was accomplished through the development of technology and trade.

STUDY TIPS

1. Have students make flash cards on the important terms and people listed at the beginning of each section. Students can work in pairs to test each other on the information.
2. Ask students to draw a chart comparing the cultural differences and similarities of the kingdoms of Kush and Mali.

CHAPTER 9

Chapter Tutorial

The Americas

IDENTIFYING TERMS Choose the term or name that correctly matches each definition.

_____ **1.** means of storing information   **a.** strait

_____ **2.** chief God of ancient Mexico   **b.** potlatches

_____ **3.** Indian people of the Southwest   **c.** Pueblo

_____ **4.** festive gatherings   **d.** Quetzalcoatl

_____ **5.** narrow strip of water   **e.** quipu

UNDERSTANDING MAIN IDEAS

1. How do scholars explain the arrival of people in the Americas?

_____

_____

2. Why were the A.D. 1400s difficult years on the Great Plains?

_____

_____

3. Why did the Hopewell and Mississippian peoples build mounds?

_____

_____

4. What were the religious beliefs of the Maya?

_____

_____

5. How did Incan rulers work to improve their empire?

_____

_____

REVIEWING THEMES

1. Science and Technology What ideas in astronomy, mathematics, and architectural engineering developed in Mesoamerica and Andean South America?

_____

_____

2. Geography How did climate changes allow for migration into the Western Hemisphere?

_____

_____

3. Government Why did the Aztec face revolts from the people they conquered?

_____

_____

THINKING CRITICALLY

1. Identifying Cause and Effect What role did military force and invasion play in shaping civilizations in the Western Hemisphere?

_____

_____

2. Supporting a Point of View Which civilization was more effective in dealing with conquered people, the Incas or the Aztec? Explain.

_____

_____

WRITING ABOUT HISTORY

Persuading Imagine you are a Hopewell Indian. Write a brief paragraph telling a modern archaeologist why your people built mounds.

_____

_____

_____

_____

IDENTIFYING TERMS Choose the term or name that correctly matches each definition.

e (p. 211) **1.** means of storing information   **a.** strait

d (p. 210) **2.** chief God of ancient Mexico   **b.** potlatches

c (p. 205) **3.** Indian people of the Southwest   **c.** Pueblo

b (p. 203) **4.** festive gatherings   **d.** Quetzalcoatl

a (p. 200) **5.** narrow strip of water   **e.** quipu

UNDERSTANDING MAIN IDEAS

1. How do scholars explain the arrival of people in the Americas?

Water trapped in glaciers during the Ice Age created a land bridge that Asians used to migrate to the Americas. (pp. 200–201)

2. Why were the A.D. 1400s difficult years on the Great Plains?

New peoples arrived from the north, pushing many plains peoples out of their homelands; drought made farming impossible in some places. (p. 205)

3. Why did the Hopewell and Mississippian peoples build mounds?

Possibly for burial. (p. 207)

4. What were the religious beliefs of the Maya?

They worshiped many gods; their rites were closely tied to agriculture; and they sacrificed humans. (p. 209)

5. How did Incan rulers work to improve their empire?

They built fortresses, roads, and irrigation systems. (p. 211)

REVIEWING THEMES

1. Science and Technology What ideas in astronomy, mathematics, and architectural engineering developed in Mesoamerica and Andean South America?

The prediction of solar eclipses, accurate calendars, counting systems that included zero, irrigation systems, and paved roads. (pp. 208–211)

2. Geography How did climate changes allow for migration into the Western Hemisphere?

When temperatures dropped, the Bering Strait became a land bridge called Beringia, allowing migrants to cross from northeastern Asia into the Western Hemisphere. (pp. 200–201)

3. **Government** Why did the Aztec face revolts from the people they conquered?

In the late 1400s, unrest grew among surrounding people who had been forced to pay oppressive tribute to the Aztec. (p. 210)

THINKING CRITICALLY

1. **Identifying Cause and Effect** What role did military force and invasion play in shaping civilizations in the Western Hemisphere?

Invaders pushed the Great Plains people off their land; Toltec warriors invaded Central Mexico; Aztec warriors conquered central Mexico; the Inca conquered and ruled most of the west coast of South America. (pp. 205, 208–211)

2. **Supporting a Point of View** Which civilization was more effective in dealing with conquered people, the Incas or the Aztec? Explain.

Answers may vary. Students may mention that the Inca tried to deal with regional differences. (pp. 210–211)

WRITING ABOUT HISTORY

Persuading Imagine you are a Hopewell Indian. Write a brief paragraph telling a modern archaeologist why your people built mounds.

Answers will vary.

STUDY TIPS

1. Have students identify some of the major Native American groups living in the United States today and plot their traditional homelands on a map. Tell students that many, but not all, Native Americans live on reservations.

2. Ask students the Read to Discover questions listed at the beginning of each section. If the students have trouble answering them, help them find the corresponding portions of the text and reread them.

Chapter Tutorial

Modern Chapter **1**

The Byzantine Empire and Russia

IDENTIFYING TERMS Choose the term or name that correctly matches each definition.

_____ **1.** collection of laws   **a.** steppe

_____ **2.** holy picture   **b.** taiga

_____ **3.** grassy plain   **c.** Justinian Code

_____ **4.** agricultural region   **d.** icon

_____ **5.** caesar   **e.** czar

UNDERSTANDING MAIN IDEAS

1. Why was the Justinian Code important?

_____

_____

2. What was the result of the Iconoclastic Controversy?

_____

_____

3. How did the Slavs benefit from the Vikings' travels in the southern part of eastern Europe?

_____

_____

4. Which rulers helped make Moscow a major city?

_____

_____

5. Why did the Russian Orthodox Church call Moscow the "third Rome?"

_____

_____

Chapter 10 Tutorial, continued

REVIEWING THEMES

1. Government Did Kievan Russia have a form of government in which citizens had a voice? Explain.

_____

_____

2. Geography What effects did access to bodies of water have on the Byzantine Empire in Kievan Russia?

_____

_____

3. Global Relations Which lasted longer, Mongol rule in Russia, or the Byzantine Empire? How did the way these two powers ruled make a difference?

_____

_____

THINKING CRITICALLY

1. Analyzing Information The Mongols in Russia were concerned with increasing their wealth by collecting taxes. Why did they work to improve the roads?

_____

_____

2. Comparing What similar factors contributed to the wealth of the Byzantine Empire and Kievan Russia?

_____

_____

WRITING ABOUT HISTORY

Describing Write a paragraph on why Ivan the Terrible was such a cruel, yet successful, leader.

_____

_____

_____

_____

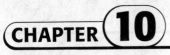

Chapter Tutorial

The Byzantine Empire and Russia

IDENTIFYING TERMS Choose the term or name that correctly matches each definition.

_c (p. 222)_ **1.** collection of laws   **a.** steppe

_d (p. 224)_ **2.** holy picture   **b.** taiga

_a (p. 229)_ **3.** grassy plain   **c.** Justinian Code

_b (p. 231)_ **4.** agricultural region   **d.** icon

_e (p. 234)_ **5.** caesar   **e.** czar

UNDERSTANDING MAIN IDEAS

1. Why was the Justinian Code important?

The Code preserved the Roman idea that people should be ruled by laws rather than by the whims of leaders. This is the basis of English civil law, one of the major legal systems in the world today. (p. 222)

2. What was the result of the Iconoclastic Controversy?

In A.D. 726, Emperor Leo ordered the destruction of icons, but many people refused to give them up. Many people in western Europe could not read or write, and icons portrayed images and symbols that helped them learn about Christianity. In A.D. 787, the church council decided that not allowing the use of icons was a heresy. (p. 226)

3. How did the Slavs benefit from the Vikings' travels in the southern part of eastern Europe?

They benefited from Viking trade. (p. 229)

4. Which rulers helped make Moscow a major city?

Ivan I, Ivan III, and Ivan the Terrible (p. 234)

5. Why did the Russian Orthodox Church call Moscow the "third Rome?"

They believed that Moscow would bring the spiritual light of Othodox Christianity to the whole world. (p. 235)

REVIEWING THEMES

1. Government Did Kievan Russia have a form of government in which citizens had a voice? Explain.

Yes. They participated in town meetings. When the Prince requested it, all heads of households would meet in the public marketplace. They discussed important matters such as wars, disputes between princes, or emergencies. (p. 231)

2. Geography What effects did access to bodies of water have on the Byzantine Empire in Kievan Russia?

It allowed them both to engage in profitable trade. (p. 230)

3. Global Relations Which lasted longer, Mongol rule in Russia, or the Byzantine Empire? How did the way these two powers ruled make a difference?

The Byzantine Empire lasted longer. It had a strong central government. Independently, the Mongol princes became weaker. (p. 233)

THINKING CRITICALLY

1. Analyzing Information The Mongols in Russia were concerned with increasing their wealth by collecting taxes. Why did they work to improve the roads?

Roads made the movement of people, goods, and armies easier. (p. 233)

2. Comparing What similar factors contributed to the wealth of the Byzantine Empire and Kievan Russia?

Their location along waterways and the ability to engage in profitable trade. (pp. 233–235)

WRITING ABOUT HISTORY

Describing Write a paragraph on why Ivan the Terrible was such a cruel, yet successful, leader.

Answers will vary. (p. 234)

STUDY TIPS

1. Have students locate and trace the Black Sea, Baltic Sea, Mediterranean Sea, Bosporus, Nile River, and Volga River. Identify cities along each waterway and the goods that were traded.

2. Ask students the Read to Discover questions listed at the beginning of each section. If the students have trouble answering them, help them find the corresponding portions of the text and reread them.

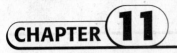

CHAPTER 11

Modern Chapter **2**

Chapter Tutorial

The Islamic World

IDENTIFYING TERMS Choose the term or name that correctly matches each definition.

_____ **1.** founder of Islam

_____ **2.** holy book of Islam

_____ **3.** place of Islamic worship

_____ **4.** Muslims from Spain

_____ **5.** successor to the Prophet

a. mosque

b. Muhammad

c. Moors

d. caliph

e. Qur'an

UNDERSTANDING MAIN IDEAS

1. Why do Muslims call Muhammad "the Prophet of Islam?"

_____

_____

2. What role does the Qur'an play in the lives of faithful Muslims?

_____

_____

3. Which areas were included in the Muslim Empire by A.D. 750?

_____

_____

4. What factors caused Islam to divide into two main branches?

_____

_____

5. Why did Muslims produce the type of art they did?

_____

_____

Chapter 11 Tutorial, continued

REVIEWING THEMES

1. Science and Technology Why was there a development and flow of scientific information in the Muslim Empire?

_____

_____

2. Global Relations How did conquest contribute to the spread of Muslim culture?

_____

_____

3. Culture In what ways did the Islamic religion shape how the Muslim culture developed?

_____

_____

THINKING CRITICALLY

1. Evaluating How did *The Thousand and One Nights* reflect both the history of the culture in which it was created and a universal theme?

_____

_____

2. Supporting a Point of View What do you think was the most important contribution of the Muslim Empire to the world? Why?

_____

_____

WRITING ABOUT HISTORY

Imagining Imagine you are a doctor of the Islamic Empire. Write a brief paragraph detailing your advances in medicine.

_____

_____

_____

IDENTIFYING TERMS Choose the term or name that correctly matches each definition.

_b (p. 241)_ **1.** founder of Islam   **a.** mosque

_e (p. 242)_ **2.** holy book of Islam   **b.** Muhammad

_a (p. 242)_ **3.** place of Islamic worship   **c.** Moors

_c (p. 245)_ **4.** Muslims from Spain   **d.** caliph

_d (p. 243)_ **5.** successor to the Prophet   **e.** Qur'an

UNDERSTANDING MAIN IDEAS

1. Why do Muslims call Muhammad "the Prophet of Islam?"

When he was 40 years old, Muhammad reported that he was visited by an angel who called him to be a prophet of God and revealed verses he was to recite. He was also instructed to teach others. (p. 241)

2. What role does the Qur'an play in the lives of faithful Muslims?

It gives them rules by which to live both their religious and private lives. (p. 242)

3. Which areas were included in the Muslim Empire by A.D. 750?

Muhammad died in A.D. 632; almost 120 years after his death the Muslim Empire included parts of Syria, Persia, North Africa, parts of India, islands in the Mediterranean Sea, and Spain. (pp. 243–245)

4. What factors caused Islam to divide into two main branches?

From the beginning, people could not agree on who should be caliph. Eventually, those disagreements split the Muslim community into two factions, the Sunni and the Shi'ah. (p. 244)

5. Why did Muslims produce the type of art they did?

Islamic teaching forbids religious images to include pictures of God, animals, or human forms. In nonreligious art, people were sometimes shown in daily life or battle. (p. 252)

REVIEWING THEMES

1. Science and Technology Why was there a development and flow of scientific information in the Muslim Empire?

Muslims exchanged information with other cultures, including cultures they traded with and cultures they conquered. (p. 248)

2. Global Relations How did conquest contribute to the spread of Muslim culture?

The people conquered by the Muslims often adopted Islamic culture. (p. 243)

3. **Culture** In what ways did the Islamic religion shape how the Muslim culture developed?

It guided both their religious life and daily life; there was no separation. (p. 249)

THINKING CRITICALLY

1. **Evaluating** How did *The Thousand and One Nights* reflect both the history of the culture in which it was created and a universal theme?

It deals with universal themes (i.e., faithfulness) within an Islamic context (i.e., many wives). (p. 258)

2. **Supporting a Point of View** What do you think was the most important contribution of the Muslim Empire to the world? Why?

Answers will vary. (pp. 248–258)

WRITING ABOUT HISTORY

Imagining Imagine you are a doctor in the Muslim Empire. Write a brief paragraph detailing your advances in medicine.

Students may write about developments in hygiene and pharmacology. (p. 25)

STUDY TIPS

1. Have students write an outline for a short story or folktale that takes place in the Muslim Empire, considering the themes in *The Thousand and One Nights*.

2. Ask students to diagram Islamic teachings and write how they affect everyday life.

Name _____ Class _____ Date _____

Modern Chapter **3**

Chapter Tutorial
The Civilizations of East Asia

IDENTIFYING TERMS Choose the term or name that correctly matches each definition.

_____ **1.** way of the kami   **a.** Marco Polo

_____ **2.** warrior   **b.** Shinto

_____ **3.** great names   **c.** shogun

_____ **4.** Italian explorer   **d.** samurai

_____ **5.** general   **e.** daimyo

UNDERSTANDING MAIN IDEAS

1. What were the most important developments in Chinese culture during the Sui, Tang, and Sung dynasties?

_____

_____

2. How did China change under Mongol rule?

_____

_____

3. How did Japan's geography affect its relations with its neighbors?

_____

_____

4. How did China influence Japanese society and culture?

_____

_____

5. What were the influences of China and India on societies in Korea and Southeast Asia?

_____

_____

Chapter 12 Tutorial, continued

REVIEWING THEMES

1. Global Relations How did proximity to China affect the rest of Asian culture?

_____

_____

_____

2. Culture How were the various forms of Buddhism reflected in east Asian culture?

_____

_____

_____

THINKING CRITICALLY

1. Drawing Influences How did the Sung and Tang dynasties change China?

_____

_____

_____

2. Contrasting How did the culture of feudal Japan differ from earlier Japanese culture?

_____

_____

_____

WRITING ABOUT HISTORY

Persuading Write a paragraph explaining how life changed for the ordinary people during the Sung dynasty.

_____

_____

_____

IDENTIFYING TERMS Choose the term or name that correctly matches each definition.

_b (p. 277)_ **1.** way of the kami   **a.** Marco Polo

_d (p. 278)_ **2.** warrior   **b.** Shinto

_e (p. 280)_ **3.** great names   **c.** shogun

_a (p. 274)_ **4.** Italian explorer   **d.** samurai

_c (p. 278)_ **5.** general   **e.** daimyo

UNDERSTANDING MAIN IDEAS

1. What were the most important developments in Chinese culture during the Sui, Tang, and Sung dynasties?

Sui: new waterways; Tang: literature, Zen Buddhism, and Confucianism; Sung: cultural and artistic progress. (pp. 266–271)

2. How did China change under Mongol rule?

A century of war ended, the population began to grow, trade and communications improved, and there was economic growth. However, heavy taxes and frequent demands for tribute by the emperor created resentment and helped to undermine Yuan authority. (pp. 274–275)

3. How did Japan's geography affect its relations with its neighbors?

The seas surrounding Japan protected the islands from foreign influences. (p. 276)

4. How did China influence Japanese society and culture?

The Japanese adopted Chinese writing and Buddhism. The art, science, government, and fashion of Japan was heavily influenced by China. In 702, the Japanese government issued a new law code modeled on Tang dynasty laws. (p. 278)

5. What were the influences of China and India on societies in Korea and Southeast Asia?

The Chinese gave them better agriculture, philosophies, and political structure; India gave them Hinduism and Buddhism. (pp. 280–283)

REVIEWING THEMES

1. Global Relations How did proximity to China affect the rest of Asian culture?

All Asian cultures were heavily influenced by China. (pp. 278–282)

2. Culture How were the various forms of Buddhism reflected in east Asian culture?

Buddhism and later, Zen Buddhism, became part of Japanese culture. Korea accepted Buddhist philosophy, and Vietnam adopted Mahayana Buddhism from China. (pp. 277–283)

THINKING CRITICALLY

1. Drawing Inferences How did the Sung and Tang dynasties change China?

The Chinese civil service system was perfected, and important innovations in the use of gunpowder and printing were made. Farming methods were improved, and heavy taxation was implemented. (p. 270)

2. Contrasting How did the culture of feudal Japan differ from earlier Japanese culture?

After the 800s, the political system in Japan that had been adapted from the Chinese began to decline. In its place, Japan developed a system of localized power. (p. 278)

WRITING ABOUT HISTORY

Persuading Write a paragraph explaining how life changed for the ordinary people during the Sung dynasty.

Students may write about how farming methods were improved, but taxes forced some peasants to become tenant farmers; poverty and overcrowding were problems in the cities. (pp. 266–271)

STUDY TIPS

1. Have students write a brief paragraph explaining how a samurai's life and duties compared to those of the American cowboy.

2. Ask students to draw a diagram that outlines the successes versus the problems of the Sui dynasty.

CHAPTER 13

Modern Chapter 4

Chapter Tutorial

The Rise of the Middle Ages

IDENTIFYING TERMS Choose the term or name that correctly matches each definition.

_____ 1. recipient of a land grant   **a.** feudalism

_____ 2. grant of land   **b.** fief

_____ 3. code of conduct   **c.** vassal

_____ 4. local political organization   **d.** chivalry

_____ 5. Great Charter   **e.** Magna Carta

UNDERSTANDING MAIN IDEAS

1. How did Magna Carta change the way England was governed?

_____

_____

2. How were feudal lords and peasants affected by the principles of chivalry?

_____

_____

3. What overall effect did Benedict have on the development of monasticism?

_____

_____

4. Why are the years 1066 and 1215 significant to English history?

_____

_____

5. Why was Otto's rule different from the Capetians' rule in France?

_____

_____

_____

_____

REVIEWING THEMES

1. Government How could religious leaders and kings have avoided many years of war in the Middle Ages?

_____

_____

2. Culture How did the practice of primogeniture exclude women or peasants from controlling land?

_____

_____

3. Economics When would working the land for the lord of a manor not have provided a living for a peasant?

_____

_____

THINKING CRITICALLY

1. Analyzing Information Why did the Concordat of Worms not end the struggles between popes and emperors?

_____

_____

2. Identifying Cause and Effect How did church officials, such as bishops, become involved in feudalism?

_____

_____

WRITING ABOUT HISTORY

Point of View Write a paragraph detailing the life of a peasant under the feudal system.

_____

_____

_____

_____

IDENTIFYING TERMS Choose the term or name that correctly matches each definition.

_c (p. 294)_ **1.** recipient of a land grant   **a.** feudalism

_b (p. 294)_ **2.** grant of land   **b.** fief

_d (p. 298)_ **3.** code of conduct   **c.** vassal

_a (p. 294)_ **4.** local political organization   **d.** chivalry

_e (p. 306)_ **5.** Great Charter   **e.** Magna Carta

UNDERSTANDING MAIN IDEAS

1. How did Magna Carta change the way England was governed?

It protected the liberties of nobles; promised no taxes without the consent of the Great Council; nobles were allowed to advise the King, and he promised not to take property without paying for it; and a person was to be judged by a jury of his peers. (p. 306)

2. How were feudal lords and peasants affected by the principles of chivalry?

Chivalry did much to improve the rough and crude manners of early feudal lords. A knight was required to extend courtesy to only people of his own class, however. Towards other classes, his attitudes and actions could be coarse and bullying, although he was expected to be courteous to women and the less powerful. (p. 299)

3. What overall effect did Benedict have on the development of monasticism?

He created rules to govern monks' lives. Monasteries and convents all over Europe adopted these standards, calling them the Benedictine Rule. (p. 301)

4. Why are the years 1066 and 1215 significant to English history?

In a decisive battle, Duke William of Normandy defeated Harold of Wessex's army at Hastings. In October 1066, William the Conqueror was crowned King of England. In 1215, a powerful group of lords joined against King John and forced him to accept a document known as Magna Carta. (pp. 305–306)

5. Why was Otto's rule different from the Capetians' rule in France?

He built a strong kingdom in Germany but was also interested in seizing control of Italy. (p. 310)

REVIEWING THEMES

1. Government How could religious leaders and kings have avoided many years of war in the Middle Ages?

By agreeing to separate matters of church and state. (pp. 311–313)

2. Culture How did the practice of primogeniture exclude women or peasants from controlling land?

Land was inherited by the eldest son of a vassal. If a woman had property, it passed to her husband upon marriage, and she could regain control of her property only if her husband died. Peasants could not own or inherit land. (p. 294)

3. Economics When would working the land for the lord of a manor not have provided a living for a peasant?

If the lord demanded all the crops the peasant produced. (p. 298)

THINKING CRITICALLY

1. Analyzing Information Why did the Concordat of Worms not end the struggles between popes and emperors?

The emperors continued to threaten the pope's rule. The popes firmly opposed the emperors' attempts to seize power in Italy. (p. 312)

2. Identifying Cause and Effect How did church officials, such as bishops, become involved in feudalism?

Many bishops were feudal lords in their own right and had vassals themselves. (p. 301)

WRITING ABOUT HISTORY

Point of View Write a paragraph detailing the life of a peasant under the feudal system.

Answers will vary. Students may write about the long hours and hard work required of the peasant for little or no reward. (pp. 297–298)

STUDY TIPS

1. Have students write a paragraph explaining the relationship between the church and nobility.

2. Ask students to draw a diagram comparing how the lot of medieval noblewomen compares to that of modern American women.

Name _____ Class _____ Date _____

IDENTIFYING TERMS Choose the term or name that correctly matches each definition.

_____ **1.** wealth saved and invested   **a.** Crusades

_____ **2.** exchange system   **b.** barter economy

_____ **3.** everyday speech   **c.** capital

_____ **4.** military expeditions to the Holy Land   **d.** vernacular language

_____ **5.** bringing together faith and reason   **e.** scholasticism

UNDERSTANDING MAIN IDEAS

1. How did the Crusades affect the government, economy, and culture of Europe?

_____

_____

2. How did the revival of trade help in the development of manufacturing, banking, and investing?

_____

_____

3. How did life for people in towns change in the late Middle Ages?

_____

_____

4. How did education, philosophy, and architecture change in the late Middle Ages?

_____

_____

5. What events led to the weakening of the Catholic Church during the late Middle Ages?

_____

_____

Chapter 14 Tutorial, continued

REVIEWING THEMES

1. Economics How did the Crusades promote an exchange of ideas and goods?

_____

_____

2. Global Relations How did the growth of trade and towns bring changes to the feudal and manorial systems?

_____

_____

3. Government What groups lost power as Europe's kings established strong nations?

_____

_____

THINKING CRITICALLY

1. Finding the Main Idea Why did the power of the Catholic Church begin to weaken after Pope Innocent III?

_____

_____

2. Summarizing What were the main advances in literature during the late Middle Ages?

_____

_____

WRITING ABOUT HISTORY

Imagining Imagine you are a young person in the Middle Ages who wants work. Write a paragraph on how a guild might help you.

_____

_____

_____

CHAPTER 14

IDENTIFYING TERMS Choose the term or name that correctly matches each definition.

_c (p. 326)_ **1.** wealth saved and invested   **a.** Crusades

_b (p. 325)_ **2.** exchange system   **b.** barter economy

_d (p. 331)_ **3.** everyday speech   **c.** capital

_a (p. 318)_ **4.** military expeditions to the Holy Land   **d.** vernacular language

_e (p. 334)_ **5.** bringing together faith and reason   **e.** scholasticism

UNDERSTANDING MAIN IDEAS

1. How did the Crusades affect the government, economy, and culture of Europe?

Kings grew stronger and levied more taxes, helping to bring an end to feudalism. Ideas were exchanged that enriched the culture, and Italian cities became large trading centers. (p. 322)

2. How did the revival of trade help in the development of manufacturing, banking, and investing?

The domestic system developed to meet the demand for goods; banks lent money and provided bills of exchange. Investors demanded profits from increased trade. (pp. 323–326)

3. How did life for people in towns change in the late Middle Ages?

Merchant and craft guilds formed and many serfs moved to towns. Some lords granted townspeople a charter of liberties stating that anyone who lived in town for a year and a day became free; they were free from having to work on the manor; they had their own courts and tried their own cases; and they could sell goods freely in the town market. (pp. 327–328)

4. How did education, philosophy, and architecture change in the late Middle Ages?

Universities developed; scholars tried to bring together faith and logic in scholasticism; Romanesque church architecture gave way to the Gothic architectural style. (pp. 333–335)

5. What events led to the weakening of the Catholic Church during the late Middle Ages?

The conflict between the French king and the pope, the Babylonian Captivity, the Great Schism, and criticism from scholars. (pp. 341–343)

REVIEWING THEMES

1. Economics How did the Crusades promote an exchange of ideas and goods?

When the Crusaders traveled to the Middle East, they were introduced to new ideas and goods, which they brought back to Europe with them. (p. 322)

2. **Global Relations** How did the growth of trade and towns bring changes to the feudal and manorial systems?

Manors were no longer self sufficient, and power shifted from the feudal lords to merchants and kings. (p. 327)

3. **Government** What groups lost power as Europe's kings established strong nations?

The nobles and the church (p. 341)

THINKING CRITICALLY

1. **Finding the Main Idea** Why did the power of the Catholic Church begin to weaken after Pope Innocent III?

Power shifted as the European kings formed strong governments and the townspeople gave them more importance. Many people felt that church laws limited trade and industry. Also, people began to question some church practices such as its method of raising money and the worldly lives of some of its clergy. (p. 341)

2. **Summarizing** What were the main advances in literature during the late Middle Ages?

There was a surge in vernacular literature, such as poems by troubadors, romances, fabliaux, epics, and drama. (pp. 331–333)

WRITING ABOUT HISTORY

Imagining Imagine you are a young person in the Middle Ages who wanted work. Write a paragraph on how a guild might help you.

Answers will vary. (p. 328)

STUDY TIPS

1. Have students explain the impact of the Black Death on Europe. Ask them to draw a time line outlining how the Black Death spread across the continent.

2. Ask students to list the ways languages and literature, education, and architecture changed during the Middle Ages.

Chapter Tutorial

CHAPTER 15
Modern Chapter 6

The Renaissance and Reformation

IDENTIFYING TERMS Choose the term or name that correctly matches each definition.

_____ **1.** defined official church doctrine

_____ **2.** contained predictions about weather

_____ **3.** government ruled by religious leaders

_____ **4.** rebirth

_____ **5.** specialist in the humanities

a. humanist

b. theocracy

c. Renaissance

d. Council of Trent

e. almanac

UNDERSTANDING MAIN IDEAS

1. What were the main values that generally characterized the Italian humanists?

_____

_____

2. How did northern Europeans learn about the Italian Renaissance?

_____

_____

3. What role did the sale of indulgences by the Catholic Church play in the Reformation?

_____

_____

4. How did the Reformation and the Counter-Reformation affect education?

_____

_____

5. What factor was mainly responsible for the decline of traditional culture?

_____

_____

Chapter 15 Tutorial, continued

REVIEWING THEMES

1. Global Relations What effect did the ideas of Martin Luther and other religious reformers have on the relations between different groups in Europe?

_____

_____

_____

2. Science, Technology and Society What effect did the printing press have on the ways in which Europeans understood their world?

_____

_____

_____

3. Culture How did the classical literature of Greece and Rome influence the development of humanism?

_____

_____

_____

THINKING CRITICALLY

1. Finding the Main Idea What was the purpose behind the Inquisition in Rome?

_____

_____

2. Supporting a Point of View How effective were the reforms of the Counter-Reformation?

_____

_____

_____

WRITING ABOUT HISTORY

Sequencing What were the main events of the Reformation and Counter-Reformation?

_____

_____

_____

_____

CHAPTER 15
Modern Chapter 6

Chapter Tutorial
The Renaissance and Reformation

IDENTIFYING TERMS Choose the term or name that correctly matches each definition.

_d (p. 369)_ **1.** defined official church doctrine

_e (p. 375)_ **2.** contained predictions about weather

_b (p. 367)_ **3.** government ruled by religious leaders

_c (p. 354)_ **4.** rebirth

_a (p. 355)_ **5.** specialist in the humanities

a. humanist

b. theocracy

c. Renaissance

d. Council of Trent

e. almanac

UNDERSTANDING MAIN IDEAS

1. What were the main values that generally characterized the Italian humanists?

They believed it was important to understand how things worked and emphasized education. They also maintained that a person should lead a meaningful life, should be active in practical affairs, and support the arts. (p. 355)

2. How did northern Europeans learn about the Italian Renaissance?

Mountain passages allowed people and ideas to pass from Italy to northern Europe, and the printing press helped make information more widely available. (p. 359)

3. What role did the sale of indulgences by the Catholic Church play in the Reformation?

Indulgences were originally a reward for pious deeds. Renaissance popes, however, sold indulgences to raise money for the church. The misuse of indulgences outraged northern humanists who wanted the church to become more spiritual. This opposition helped fuel the Reformation. (p. 364)

4. How did the Reformation and the Counter-Reformation affect education?

Education and reading became more important and more universities were created. (p. 371)

5. What factor was mainly responsible for the decline of traditional culture?

The movement of people from countryside to city. (p. 377)

REVIEWING THEMES

1. Global Relations What effect did the ideas of Martin Luther and other religious reformers have on the relations between different groups in Europe?

They led to conflict. (p. 365)

2. Science, Technology and Society What effect did the printing press have on the ways in which Europeans understood their world?

It hastened and increased the spread of knowledge and new ideas. (p. 375)

3. **Culture** How did the classical literature of Greece and Rome influence the development of humanism?

It was a main feature of Renaissance humanist thought. (p. 355)

THINKING CRITICALLY

1. **Finding the Main Idea** What was the purpose behind the Inquisition in Rome?

In the past, governments had used extreme punishments against criminals. The church began to use similar punishments to keep Catholics within the church and to combat heresy. (p. 368)

2. **Supporting a Point of View** How effective were the reforms of the Counter-Reformation?

The Catholic Church clarified doctrines and fostered spirituality, but religious conflict continued to grow. (pp. 368–371)

WRITING ABOUT HISTORY

Sequencing What were the main events of the Reformation and Counter-Reformation?

Luther's 95 theses, Luther's excommunication, establishment of Lutheran Church, Peace of Augsburg, creation of Anglican Church, founding of Calvinisim, Edict of Nantes, Inquisition in Rome, Index of Forbidden Books, Council of Trent, establishment of the Jesuit order. (pp. 363–371)

STUDY TIPS

1. Have students write a paragraph with several theses to persuade people that the sale of indulgences is wrong.

2. Have students diagram the events in the daily lives of peasants that led to their superstitious beliefs.

CHAPTER 16

Modern Chapter 7

Chapter Tutorial

Exploration and Expansion

IDENTIFYING TERMS Choose the term or name that correctly matches each definition.

_____ **1.** period between the late 1400s and 1700s

_____ **2.** tax on imports

_____ **3.** system of trade involving slavery

_____ **4.** Earth-centered theory

_____ **5.** sun-centered theory

a. geocentric

b. heliocentric

c. Commercial Revolution

d. tariff

e. triangular trade

UNDERSTANDING MAIN IDEAS

1. What were some of the important scientific discoveries made during this period?

_____

_____

2. What changes in science and economics made European exploration possible?

_____

_____

3. What were some of the factors leading to the Atlantic slave trade?

_____

_____

4. What new knowledge did early Portuguese explorers provide that increased successful exploration?

_____

_____

5. What factors led to the decline of the Spanish Empire?

_____

_____

Chapter 16 Tutorial, continued

REVIEWING THEMES

1. Science, Technology and, Society How did the era known as the Scientific Revolution lead to developments in other areas of society?

_____

_____

2. Economics How did the theory of mercantilism influence nations' decisions to explore and colonize?

_____

_____

3. Global Relations What determined the kinds of relationships that European exploreres formed with conquered peoples?

_____

_____

THINKING CRITICALLY

1. Sequencing Trace the events leading to the rise and decline of the Spanish Empire.

_____

_____

2. Supporting a Point of View Which European nations that engaged in exploration, trade, and colonization during the Age of Exploration had the greatest effect on other peoples? Explain.

_____

_____

WRITING ABOUT HISTORY

Persuading Following the idea of Descartes that no assumptions should be made without questions, write a paragraph questioning the geocentric theory.

_____

_____

IDENTIFYING TERMS Choose the term or name that correctly matches each definition.

_c (p. 389)_ **1.** period between the late 1400s and 1700s

_d (p. 390)_ **2.** tax on imports

_e (p. 398)_ **3.** system of trade involving slavery

_a (p. 383)_ **4.** Earth-centered theory

_b (p. 383)_ **5.** sun-centered theory

a. geocentric

b. heliocentric

c. Commercial Revolution

d. tariff

e. triangular trade

UNDERSTANDING MAIN IDEAS

1. What were some of the important scientific discoveries made during this period?

   The Earth moves around the sun; laws of planetary motion, universal gravitation, conservation of matter; circulation of blood; calculus; bacteria; and oxygen. (pp. 382–387)

2. What changes in science and economics made European exploration possible?

   The invention of the compass and astrolabe, standardization of money, and establishment of joint-stock companies. (pp. 388–389)

3. What were some of the factors leading to the Atlantic slave trade?

   European demand for labor in the American colonies and the devastation of the American Indian population by European diseases. (p. 395)

4. What new knowledge did early Portuguese explorers provide that increased successful exploration?

   They discovered that Asia was accessible by sea by going around the southern tip of Africa. (p. 392)

5. What factors led to the decline of the Spanish Empire?

   Inflation caused by an influx of gold and silver, industrial decline, the lack of a middle class, and expulsion of the Jews and Moriscos. (p. 407)

REVIEWING THEMES

1. **Science, Technology, and Society** How did the era known as the Scientific Revolution lead to developments in other areas of society?

   The new scientific ways of thinking about the world led to less acceptance of old beliefs. There was new technology for maritime exploration, making expansion possible. (pp. 387–389)

2. Economics How did the theory of mercantilism influence nations' decisions to explore and colonize?

Mercantilism led to the desire for gold and silver and the idea of using the colonies as sources of raw materials and markets for manufactured items. (p. 390)

3. Global Relations What determined the kinds of relationships that European explorers formed with conquered peoples?

Whether or not colonists tried to enslave the native peoples (pp. 392–399)

THINKING CRITICALLY

1. Sequencing Trace the events leading to the rise and decline of the Spanish Empire.

Isabella and Ferdinand unite Spain and sponsor Columbus; the expulsion of the Jews and Moriscos; Cortés conquers the Aztecs; Pizarro conquers the Incas; Spanish settlements are established in the Americas; Phillip II loses the Netherlands. (pp. 393–407)

2. Supporting a Point of View Which European nations that engaged in exploration, trade, and colonization during the Age of Exploration had the greatest effect on other peoples? Explain.

Spain because of the devastation of the American Indian population by the diseases carried by Spanish explorers, (p. 401) and Portugal because they became the leaders of the slave trade. (p. 395)

WRITING ABOUT HISTORY

Persuading Following the idea of Descartes that no assumptions should be made without questions, write a paragraph questioning the geocentric theory.

Answers will vary.

STUDY TIPS

1. Have students write a paragraph outlining triangular trade.

2. Ask students to look at the map on page 398 and approximate how many miles the trip was for a slave from Africa to the New World.

CHAPTER 17

Modern Chapter 8

Chapter Tutorial

Asia in Transition

IDENTIFYING TERMS Choose the term or name that correctly matches each definition.

_____ **1.** U.S. Navy commodore

_____ **2.** Chinese ships

_____ **3.** diplomatic offices

_____ **4.** history of literature and language

_____ **5.** 1854 U.S. agreement with Japan

a. junks

b. philology

c. Matthew Perry

d. consulates

e. Treaty of Kanagawa

UNDERSTANDING MAIN IDEAS

1. Why did the Chinese abandon overseas exploration?

_____

_____

2. Why did the British government favor free trade with China?

_____

_____

3. What generally were the terms of "unequal" treaties?

_____

_____

4. Why did Japanese rulers see the Jesuits as a threat?

_____

_____

5. Why did Japan open its ports to American ships?

_____

_____

REVIEWING THEMES

1. Global Relations Why did Chinese and Japanese efforts to maintain isolation fail in the 1800s?

_____

_____

2. Economics How did attitudes about foreigners affect trade in China?

_____

_____

3. Government What was the result of the Qing dynasty's loss of control over bureaucratic corruption and inability to provide services?

_____

_____

THINKING CRITICALLY

1. Evaluating What were the main difficulties that Asian societies faced during this period in history?

_____

_____

2. Making Predictions What might have happened if the Qing dynasty had improved tax reform and increased government services?

_____

_____

WRITING ABOUT HISTORY

Persuading Using the quotation on page 429, explain why you think Francis Xavier, the Jesuit, was so taken with the Japanese people?

_____

_____

_____

IDENTIFYING TERMS Choose the term or name that correctly matches each definition.

_c (p. 426)_ **1.** U.S. Navy commodore

_a (p. 412)_ **2.** Chinese ships

_d (p. 427)_ **3.** diplomatic offices

_b (p. 415)_ **4.** history of literature and language

_e (p. 427)_ **5.** 1854 U.S. agreement with Japan

a. junks

b. philology

c. Matthew Perry

d. consulates

e. Treaty of Kanagawa

UNDERSTANDING MAIN IDEAS

1. Why did the Chinese abandon overseas exploration?

The Ming emperors wanted China to be self-sufficient. They refused to rely on foreign trade as a source of government revenue. They focused their efforts on strengthening the long northern frontier. (p. 413)

2. Why did the British government favor free trade with China?

The British government hoped to gain additional overseas markets for British goods. (p. 418)

3. What generally were the terms of "unequal" treaties?

Most of the benefits of these treaties went to the foreign powers. (p. 419)

4. Why did Japanese rulers see the Jesuits as a threat?

The shoguns thought Christianity would weaken their authority because it taught loyalty to a power other than the shogun. (p. 424)

5. Why did Japan open its ports to American ships?

They were forced to sign the Treaty of Kanagawa by the threat of U. S. naval forces. (p. 427)

REVIEWING THEMES

1. Global Relations Why did Chinese and Japanese efforts to maintain isolation fail in the 1800s?

Western nations insisted on establishing free trade. (pp. 417–427)

2. Economics How did attitudes about foreigners affect trade in China?

They led to limits and regulations on trade until China was forced into free trade by its defeat in the Opium War. (pp. 417–421)

3. Government What was the result of the Qing dynasty's inability to provide services and loss of control over bureaucratic corruption?

Internal rebellion and the weakening of the dynasty (pp. 412–416)

THINKING CRITICALLY

1. Evaluating What were the main difficulties that Asian societies faced during this period in history?

Western culture, isolationism, overpopulation, and the inability to adapt and change (pp. 417–427)

2. Making Predictions What might have happened if the Qing dynasty had improved tax reform and increased government services?

They might have retained power. (pp. 412–416)

WRITING ABOUT HISTORY

Persuading Using the quotation on page 429, explain why you think Francis Xavier, the Jesuit, was so taken with the Japanese people?

Answers will vary.

STUDY TIPS

1. Have students compile a list of people discussed in the chapter and rank them based on their impact on issues of trade.

2. Ask students the Read to Discover questions listed at the beginning of each section. If the students have trouble answering them, help them find the corresponding portions of the text and reread them.

CHAPTER  18

Modern Chapter **6**

Chapter Tutorial

Islamic Empires in Asia

IDENTIFYING TERMS Choose the term or name that correctly matches each definition.

_____ **1.** separate religious communities

_____ **2.** tomb of Mumtâz, Mahal

_____ **3.** Indian warrior princes

_____ **4.** princely title

_____ **5.** trained slave troops

a. Janissaries

b. millets

c. Rajputs

d. Taj Mahal

e. Aurangzeb

UNDERSTANDING MAIN IDEAS

1. Why were the Janissaries important to the Ottoman sultans?

_____

_____

2. How did the Ottoman Turks maintain peace among the various ethnic groups within their widespread empire?

_____

_____

3. How did Shi'ah Islam affect the Persians' ideas about themselves?

_____

_____

4. What events marked the beginning of the Mughal Empire?

_____

_____

5. What were Akbar's most important accomplishments?

_____

_____

Chapter 18 Tutorial, continued

REVIEWING THEMES

1. Global Relations What evidence exists that the Islamic empires supported large strong militaries?

_____

_____

2. Government How might a person's abilities influence what role he or she played in Islamic society?

_____

_____

3. Culture How did religious policies affect the Islamic empires?

_____

_____

THINKING CRITICALLY

1. Drawing Inferences In what way might the building of the Taj Mahal have contributed to the decline of the Mughal Empire?

_____

_____

2. Supporting a Point of View What evidence would you give that in the Ottoman Empire ordinary people had an equal opportunity for success?

_____

_____

WRITING ABOUT HISTORY

Opinion In your opinion, how has the influence of religion over government policy evolved since the time of the Ottoman Empire?

_____

_____

_____

IDENTIFYING TERMS Choose the term or name that correctly matches each definition.

_b (p. 434)_ **1.** separate religious communities   **a.** Janissaries

_d (p. 441)_ **2.** tomb of Mumtâz, Mahal   **b.** millets

_c (p. 439)_ **3.** Indian warrior princes   **c.** Rajputs

_e (p. 443)_ **4.** princely title   **d.** Taj Mahal

_a (p. 432)_ **5.** trained slave troops   **e.** Aurangzeb

UNDERSTANDING MAIN IDEAS

1. Why were the Janissaries important to the Ottoman sultans?

Janissaries were young captives schooled in Islamic law and converted to Islam; then they were trained as special soldiers. Janissaries belonged to the Sultan, serving him for life. Eventually, they gained power and influence and became an important political group in the Ottoman Empire. (p. 432)

2. How did the Ottoman Turks maintain peace among the various ethnic groups within their widespread empire?

They allowed the various groups to govern themselves. (p. 434)

3. How did Shi'ah Islam affect the Persians' ideas about themselves?

It gave the Persians an identity and helped them to unify. (p. 437)

4. What events marked the beginning of the Mughal Empire?

Bâbur took the town of Panipat and then took Delhi and the surrounding region. (p. 439)

5. What were Akbar's most important accomplishments?

He improved the tax system, support for the arts, toleration for all religions, and an improved economy. (p. 440)

REVIEWING THEMES

1. Global Relations What evidence exists that the Islamic empires supported large strong militaries?

The histories of the Janissaries and the kizilbash provide evidence of the importance of strong militaries in the Isalmic empires. (pp. 432–436)

2. Government How might a person's abilities influence what role he or she played in Islamic society?

People with ability could become part of the ruling class. (p. 434)

3. Culture How did religious policies affect the Islamic empires?

Tolerant policies benefited the Ottomans. Forcing subjects to accept the Shi'ah faith strengthened the Safavid Empire. In Mughal India, persecution and oppression weakened government control. (pp. 434–437, 443)

THINKING CRITICALLY

1. Drawing Inferences In what way might the building of the Taj Mahal have contributed to the decline of the Mughal Empire?

Students might say that Shah Jahan raised taxes to pay for the expenses of his military campaigns against the Persians perhaps because the building of the Taj Mahal was so expensive. (p. 441)

2. Supporting a Point of View What evidence would you give that in the Ottoman Empire ordinary people had an equal opportunity for success?

If a person had the ability, he had the opportunity to advance. (p. 434)

WRITING ABOUT HISTORY

Opinion In your opinion, how has the influence of religion over government policy evolved since the time of the Ottoman Empire?

Student opinions may vary. They may write that Christian and Islamic influences still affect many world government policies.

STUDY TIPS

1. Have students write a brief paragraph explaining why the doctrine of one God conflicted with Hinduism.

2. Ask student to draw a time line detailing the rise and fall of the Ottoman Empire.

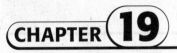

CHAPTER 19

Modern Chapter 10

Chapter Tutorial

Monarchs of Europe

IDENTIFYING TERMS Choose the term or name that correctly matches each definition.

_____ **1.** chosen by God to rule

_____ **2.** landowners without titles

_____ **3.** king of England

_____ **4.** French clergyman

_____ **5.** major reversal of alliances

a. Cardinal Richelieu

b. divine right of kings

c. Diplomatic Revolution

d. gentry

e. James I

UNDERSTANDING MAIN IDEAS

1. How did Cardinal Richelieu strengthen France?

_____

_____

2. What foreign policy successes did Catherine the Great have?

_____

_____

3. What wars did the Prussian invasion of Silesia trigger?

_____

_____

4. Why did James I clash with Parliament?

_____

_____

5. Why did Phillip II attempt to invade England? What was the result?

_____

_____

Chapter 19 Tutorial, continued

REVIEWING THEMES

1. Economics How did Peter the Great's rule affect Russian serfs?

_____

_____

2. Government How did the government of Louis XIV negatively affect the people of France?

_____

_____

3. Culture How did Elizabeth I try to control religious disunity in England?

_____

_____

THINKING CRITICALLY

1. Identifying Cause and Effect What happened to the French economy as a result of the construction of the palace at Versailles?

_____

_____

2. Comparing In what ways were Elizabeth I and James I similar?

_____

_____

WRITING ABOUT HISTORY

Opinion Write a paragraph either agreeing or disagreeing with the idea that religious beliefs have little if any effect on the degree of unity or disunity in any society.

_____

_____

_____

Modern Chapter **10**   **Monarchs of Europe**

IDENTIFYING TERMS Choose the term or name that correctly matches each definition.

_b (p. 456)_ **1.** chosen by God to rule   **a.** Cardinal Richelieu

_d (p. 472)_ **2.** landowners without titles   **b.** divine right of kings

_e (p. 473)_ **3.** king of England   **c.** Diplomatic Revolution

_a (p. 454)_ **4.** French clergyman   **d.** gentry

_c (p. 467)_ **5.** major reversal of alliances   **e.** James I

UNDERSTANDING MAIN IDEAS

1. How did Cardinal Richelieu strengthen France?

To strengthen the monarchy, Richelieu worked to take power away from the nobles and political rights away from the Huguenots. To strengthen France, he encouraged trade and industry. He also worked to keep the Thirty Years' War going while keeping France out of the fighting. Other European countries became weak from fighting while France stayed strong. (p. 455)

2. What foreign policy sucesses did Catherine the Great have?

She continued the expansion of Russia started by Peter the Great. She gained control of most of the northern shore of the Black Sea and the Crimea region as well as parts of Poland. (p. 463)

3. What wars did the Prussian invasion of Silesia trigger?

The War of Austrian Succession, which lasted from 1740 to 1746 (p. 467)

4. Why did James I clash with Parliament?

Puritans in Parliament opposed James' support of the Anglican Church. (p. 473)

5. Why did Phillip II attempt to invade England? What was the result?

Phillip was angered by the British raiders at sea and by the help Elizabeth gave to Spanish Protestants. The invasion failed. (p. 471)

REVIEWING THEMES

1. Economics How did Peter the Great's rule affect Russian serfs?

When Peter created the "service nobility", he granted individual nobles large estates with thousands of serfs. He increased the number of serfs in Russia, worsening their condition. The serfs were not only bound to the land, but also to their lords. (p. 462)

2. **Government** How did the government of Louis XIV negatively affect the people of France?

Building the palace at Versailles drained the treasury and weakened the economy. Ending the policy of tolerance for Protestants led to the loss of the Huguenots who had been productive citizens. His wars also took a toll on France's economy, creating financial strain. (pp. 455–457)

3. **Culture** How did Elizabeth I try to control religious disunity in England?

She tried to unite the population of England in the Anglican Church. (p. 471)

THINKING CRITICALLY

1. **Identifying Cause and Effect** What happened to the French economy as a result of the construction of the palace at Versailles?

The palace was so expensive to build that it weakened the French economy. (p. 455)

2. **Comparing** In what ways were Elizabeth I and James I similar?

Both were Protestants and both went to war with Spain. (pp. 470–473)

WRITING ABOUT HISTORY

Opinion Write a paragraph either agreeing or disagreeing with the idea that religious beliefs have little if any effect on the degree of unity or disunity in any society.

Answers will vary. Students may write about conflicts in societies where separation of church and state is not practiced.

STUDY TIPS

1. Have students write a paragraph explaining why the Seven Years' War might be considered the first world war. *(p. 468)*

2. Ask students to diagram the positive and negative aspects of marriage for Elizabeth I.

Modern Chapter 11

Chapter Tutorial

Enlightenment and Revolution in England and America

IDENTIFYING TERMS Choose the term or name that correctly matches each definition.

_____ **1.** granted freedoms to Dissenters

_____ **2.** document outlining basic laws

_____ **3.** tax imposed on documents

_____ **4.** republic

_____ **5.** petition stating four ancient liberties

a. Petition of Right

b. commonwealth

c. constitution

d. Toleration Act

e. Stamp Act

UNDERSTANDING MAIN IDEAS

1. What were the immediate causes of the English Revolution?

_____

_____

2. What role did religion play in English politics after the Restoration?

_____

_____

3. What was the British policy of mercantilism?

_____

_____

4. How did Enlightenment thinking affect some people's view of church and state?

_____

_____

5. What issues led to the American Revolution?

_____

_____

_____

Chapter 20 Tutorial, continued

REVIEWING THEMES

1. Citizenship How did many political writers and philosophers of the 1700s see the relationship between the people and their government?

_____

_____

2. Constitutional Heritage What were the sources of the political ideas that led to the American Revolution and the U. S. Constitution?

_____

_____

_____

3. Global Relations Why did British policy anger many Americans in the years following 1763?

_____

_____

_____

THINKING CRITICALLY

1. Identifying Cause and Effect What features of British policy probably led Americans to design the government created by the U.S. Constitution?

_____

_____

_____

2. Supporting a Point of View Although the United States was created with the Declaration of Independence, how could it be argued that the country was really launched in 1789?

_____

_____

_____

WRITING ABOUT HISTORY

Persuading Write a brief paragraph describing the difficulties that the U.S. Congress had in building a strong army.

_____

_____

_____

_____

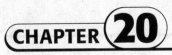
IDENTIFYING TERMS Choose the term or name that correctly matches each definition.

_d (p. 487)_ **1.** granted freedoms to Dissenters

_c (p. 481)_ **2.** document outlining basic laws

_e (p. 498)_ **3.** tax imposed on documents

_b (p. 480)_ **4.** republic

_a (p. 478)_ **5.** petition stating four ancient liberties

a. Petition of Right

b. commonwealth

c. constitution

d. Toleration Act

e. Stamp Act

UNDERSTANDING MAIN IDEAS

1. What were the immediate causes of the English Revolution?

The fear of absolute rule, the laws of Long Parliament, the Irish Rebellion, the arrest of Charles I's opponents, and religious differences. (pp. 478–482)

2. What role did religion play in English politics after the Restoration?

Charles II sought to increase tolerance for Catholics, but because of parliamentary objections, he was forced to abandon the effort. James II's efforts to help Catholics spurred Protestants to resist his rule. (pp. 483–484)

3. What was the British policy of mercantilism?

The British believed that the colonies existed for the economic benefit of the home country, and that for a nation to become wealthy, it must export more goods than it imported. They saw the colonies as sources of raw material for the factories of the home country and as markets for the products of those factories. (p. 493)

4. How did Enlightenment thinking affect some people's view of church and state?

Some thinkers downplayed the importance of religion. Enlightenment ideas about secularism and individualism would later influence some ideas about the separation of church and state in government. (p. 494)

5. What issues led to the American Revolution?

Taxation without representation and fewer rights as citizens than the British citizens in England had. (p. 498)

REVIEWING THEMES

1. Citizenship How did many political writers and philosophers of the 1700s see the relationship between the people and their government?

As adversarial. Many writers and philosophers believed that government would only be effective if it were governed by the people and for the people. They believed that the church had too much control in government, that there should be more religious freedom, and that there must be a balance of power between the branches of government. (pp. 494–496)

2. Constitutional Heritage What were the sources of the political ideas that led to the American Revolution and the U. S. Constitution?

The writings of Baron de Montesquieu, Voltaire, Jean-Jacques Rousseau, and John Locke. (pp. 495–496, 499)

3. Global Relations Why did British policy anger many Americans in the years following 1763?

After the American Indian uprising, the British barred colonists from settling west of the Appalachians and began to enforce its mercantile trade laws. They also began to impose greater taxes. (p. 498)

THINKING CRITICALLY

1. Identifying Cause and Effect What features of British policy probably led Americans to design the government created by the U.S. Constitution?

Their dislike of the monarchy and the lack of representation of the people in government (p. 499)

2. Supporting a Point of View Although the United States was created with the Declaration of Independence, how could it be argued that the country was really launched in 1789?

The U.S. Constitution was ratified and put into effect in 1789. (p. 503)

WRITING ABOUT HISTORY

Persuading Write a brief paragraph describing the difficulties that the U.S. Congress had in building a strong army.

Answers will vary. (p. 501)

STUDY TIPS

1. Have students write a paragraph outlining the effects of the Declaration of Independence.

2. Ask students to draw a chart comparing and contrasting the Articles of Confederation and the U.S. Constitution.

Name _____ Class _____ Date _____

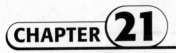

Modern Chapter 12   **The French Revolution and Napoléon**

Chapter Tutorial

IDENTIFYING TERMS Choose the term or name that correctly matches each definition.

_____ **1.** those wanting drastic changes   **a.** bourgeoisie

_____ **2.** urban middle class   **b.** radicals

_____ **3.** vote yes or no   **c.** universal manhood suffrage

_____ **4.** financial reward for damages   **d.** plebiscite

_____ **5.** every man can vote   **e.** indemnity

UNDERSTANDING MAIN IDEAS

1. What role did the meeting of the Estates General in 1789 play in bringing about the French Revolution?

_____

_____

2. Describe the accomplishments of the National Assembly.

_____

_____

3. What abilities helped Napoléon rise to power?

_____

_____

4. List three of Napoléon's most important defeats.

_____

_____

5. How did Prince Metternich react to liberalism?

_____

_____

Chapter 21 Tutorial, *continued*

REVIEWING THEMES

1. Economy What economic changes led to growing discontent?

_____

_____

2. Constitutional Heritage How did the Constitution of 1791 change the status of the French monarchy?

_____

_____

3. Citizenship How did the death of Robespierre affect the National Convention?

_____

_____

THINKING CRITICALLY

1. Finding the Main Idea How did the structure of French society lend itself to a revolution?

_____

_____

2. Comparing How was the American Revolution different from the French Revolution?

_____

_____

WRITING ABOUT HISTORY

Describing Write a paragraph describing the three estates.

_____

_____

_____

_____

IDENTIFYING TERMS Choose the term or name that correctly matches each definition.

_b (p. 515)_ **1.** those wanting drastic changes   **a.** bourgeoisie

_a (p. 509)_ **2.** urban middle class   **b.** radicals

_d (p. 523)_ **3.** vote yes or no   **c.** universal manhood suffrage

_e (p. 530)_ **4.** financial reward for damages   **d.** plebiscite

_c (p. 517)_ **5.** every man can vote   **e.** indemnity

UNDERSTANDING MAIN IDEAS

1. What role did the meeting of the Estates General in 1789 play in bringing about the French Revolution?

The representatives of the Third Estate refused to vote as one body. They argued that the Estates General represented the French people, not the three classes. The Third Estate declared itself to be the National Assembly and invited the other two estates to work with it. They declared they would not stop meeting until France had a constitution. (p. 511)

2. Describe the accomplishments of the National Assembly.

It divided France into 83 equal departments, called for the election of local officials, seized lands owned by the Catholic Church, sold them to the public, and used the proceeds to help pay off the national debt. The National Assembly gave the people the right to elect their own clergy, finished writing a constitution limiting the authority of the king, and divided the government into three branches: executive, legislative, and judicial. (pp. 513–514)

3. What abilities helped Napoléon rise to power?

He had great organizational skills and was a good manager of both political and military affairs. His smartest personal move was his marriage to Joséphine de Beauharnais. He also had a great talent for seizing public attention and for making himself popular with the French people. (pp. 521–522)

4. List three of Napoléon's most important defeats.

Students' answers may include the Peninsular War, Russia, the Leipzig Saxony War and Waterloo. (pp. 526–528)

5. How did Prince Metternich react to liberalism?

With repression (p. 533)

REVIEWING THEMES

1. Economy What economic changes led to growing discontent?

The population had grown, families had more children to support, and they needed more food and money. Land owners pushed for higher rents, and laborers found food prices rising but not wages. The poor resented the fact that the rich had more than enough to eat but did not have to pay taxes. (p. 509)

2. Constitutional Heritage How did the Constitution of 1791 change the status of the French monarchy?

It greatly limited the powers of the king. He could no longer make or block laws on his own. (p. 514)

3. Citizenship How did the death of Robespierre affect the National Convention?

The wealthy middle class took control of the National Convention after the execution of Robespierre, and in 1795, another constitution was completed allowing only male property owners to vote. (pp. 519–521)

THINKING CRITICALLY

1. Finding the Main Idea How did the structure of French society lend itself to a revolution?

A few people held all the wealth and power. Everyone else was heavily taxed and excluded from participating in government. (pp. 508–511)

2. Comparing How was the American Revolution different from the French Revolution?

The Americans were fighting against foreign control; the French fought to overthrow a monarchy. (pp. 512–516)

WRITING ABOUT HISTORY

Describing Write a paragraph describing the three estates.

Answers will vary but should include information about the three classes. (pp. 508–509)

STUDY TIPS

1. Have students write a paragraph either for or against the Reign of Terror and the repressions of Robespierre.

2. Ask students to constuct a flowchart indicating the events that led to the end of the monarchy.

CHAPTER 22

Chapter Tutorial

Modern Chapter 13

The Industrial Revolution

IDENTIFYING TERMS Choose the term or name that correctly matches each definition.

_____ **1.** complete control of a single good or service

_____ **2.** using machinery to increase production

_____ **3.** working class

_____ **4.** large group of workers stops working

_____ **5.** producing large numbers of identical items

a. mechanization

b. mass production

c. monopoly

d. strike

e. proletariat

UNDERSTANDING MAIN IDEAS

1. What were some of the important inventions and scientific discoveries of the Industrial Revolution?

_____

_____

_____

2. How did the lives of women change during the Industrial Revolution?

_____

_____

_____

3. How did methods of production change during the Industrial Revolution?

_____

_____

_____

4. What role did unions play in improving wages and working conditions?

_____

_____

_____

5. What led to the development of socialism and communism?

_____

_____

_____

Chapter 22 Tutorial, continued

REVIEWING THEMES

1. Economics What was the iron law of wages?

_____

_____

_____

2. Government What was the Factory Act of 1802 and why was it ineffective?

_____

_____

_____

3. Science, Technology, and Society How did the Industrial Revolution influence other areas of society?

_____

_____

_____

THINKING CRITICALLY

1. Making Generalizations What factors forced employers to improve wages and working conditions?

_____

_____

_____

2. Cause and Effect What is Adam Smith's law of supply and demand?

_____

_____

_____

WRITING ABOUT HISTORY

Point of View Write a paragraph explaining the ideas of Robert Owen.

_____

_____

_____

_____

_____

_____

_____

IDENTIFYING TERMS Choose the term or name that correctly matches each definition.

_c (p. 557)_ **1.** complete control of a single good or service

_a (p. 546)_ **2.** using machinery to increase production

_e (p. 566)_ **3.** working class

_d (p. 562)_ **4.** large group of workers stops working

_b (p. 556)_ **5.** producing large numbers of identical items

a. mechanization

b. mass production

c. monopoly

d. strike

e. proletariat

UNDERSTANDING MAIN IDEAS

1. What were some of the important inventions and scientific discoveries of the Industrial Revolution?

Seed drill (Jethro Tull), crop rotation (Townsend), replaceable plow blades (Jethro Wood), mechanized loom (Kay), spinning "jenny" (Hargreaves), cotton gin (Whitney), steam engine (Watt), steel (Kelly, Bessemer), and Morse code (Morse). (pp. 544–548)

2. How did the lives of women change during the Industrial Revolution?

They took factory jobs, became nurses, teachers, telephone operators, and secretaries. They also were able to attend college. Many middle-class women did not have to work and could spend more time with their children. (p. 554)

3. How did methods of production change during the Industrial Revolution?

Factory owners divided the manufacturing process into steps. They hired unskilled labor to perform each step. The use of machines in some of the steps helped the workers produce more in a shorter time. (p. 555)

4. What role did unions play in improving wages and working conditions?

Unions represented the workers to management in discussions of disputes over wages, hours, and conditions. Agreements were written into contracts lasting for a fixed period of time. Unions collected dues from workers and paid the workers from those funds when there was a strike. (p. 563)

5. What led to the development of socialism and communism?

Uneven distribution of wealth (p. 564)

REVIEWING THEMES

1. Economics What was the iron law of wages?

Ricardo stated that supply and demand determine wages. When labor is plentiful, wages remain low. When labor is scarce, wages rise. As the population grows, more workers become available and wages drop. (p. 560)

2. Government What was the Factory Act of 1802 and why was it ineffective?

The Factory Act of 1802 shortened hours and improved conditions for children working in cotton mills. It was ineffective because it had no means of enforcement. The Factory Act of 1833 corrected this omission. (p. 562)

3. Science, Technology, and Society How did the Industrial Revolution influence other areas of society?

It helped create a middle class, put women and children in the work force, and create a capitalist economy. It also gave rise to corporations and spawned ideas of social, political, and economic reform. (pp. 551–563)

THINKING CRITICALLY

1. Making Generalizations What factors forced employers to improve wages and working conditions?

Strikes, protests, competition, profit loss, and unions (pp. 559–563)

2. Cause and Effect What is Adam Smith's law of supply and demand?

Prices and profits depend on both the amount of available goods and the demand for those goods. If an item is scarce and in great demand, people pay a high price for it and profits rise. As manufacturers then invest money to make more of the product, supplies soon exceed demand, and prices go down. (p. 559)

WRITING ABOUT HISTORY

Point of View Write a paragraph explaining the ideas of Robert Owen.

Answers will vary. (p. 565)

STUDY TIPS

1. Have students write a modern example of supply and demand.

2. Ask students the Read to Discover questions listed at the beginning of each section. If the students have trouble answering, help them find the corresponding portions of the text and reread them.

Name _____ Class _____ Date _____

CHAPTER 23 Chapter Tutorial

Modern Chapter **14** **Life in the Industrial Age**

IDENTIFYING TERMS Choose the term or name that correctly matches each definition.

_____ **1.** movement of air around objects   **a.** dynamo

_____ **2.** electric generator   **b.** evolution

_____ **3.** artistic movement   **c.** aerodynamics

_____ **4.** development through change   **d.** romanticism

_____ **5.** a form of realism   **e.** regionalism

UNDERSTANDING MAIN IDEAS

1. Why did Orville and Wilbur Wright succeed where others failed?

_____

_____

2. What advances were made in atomic theory?

_____

_____

3. How did Darwin's theory of evolution influence the field of sociology?

_____

_____

4. What effect did improved food storage have on population growth?

_____

_____

5. How did the work of the postimpressionist sculptors and painters step away from realism?

_____

_____

Chapter 23 Tutorial, continued

REVIEWING THEMES

1. Citizenship How did education change during the 1800s?

_____

_____

2. Science, Technology, and Society How did electricity affect communication?

_____

_____

3. Culture How was romanticism a response to industrialized society?

_____

_____

THINKING CRITICALLY

1. Drawing Inferences How did the public education systems that developed in France and the United States help to fulfill the ideas of equality and a representative government?

_____

_____

2. Making Predictions How might innovations in transportation and communication affect social mobility?

_____

_____

WRITING ABOUT HISTORY

Imagining Imagine that you were born before the invention of the telephone. Write a paragraph describing how you might have communicated with friends and family.

_____

_____

_____

IDENTIFYING TERMS Choose the term or name that correctly matches each definition.

c (p. 575) **1.** movement of air around objects   **a.** dynamo

a (p. 572) **2.** electric generator   **b.** evolution

d (p. 592) **3.** artistic movement   **c.** aerodynamics

b (p. 577) **4.** development through change   **d.** romanticism

e (p. 596) **5.** a form of realism   **e.** regionalism

UNDERSTANDING MAIN IDEAS

1. Why did Orville and Wilbur Wright succeed where others failed?

The Wright brothers succeeded by combining science with technology. They studied the science of aerodynamics and the technology of internal combustion engines to propel their plane through the air. (p. 575)

2. What advances were made in atomic theory?

Dalton designed a method to weigh atoms; Mendeleyev made the first periodic table; the Curies discovered radioactivity; Rutherford identified the nucleus; Planck developed quantum theory; and Einstein developed his special theory of relativity. (pp. 580–582)

3. How did Darwin's theory of evolution influence the field of sociology?

Herbert Spencer applied Darwin's theory of natural selection to human societies, coining the phrase "survival of the fittest." (p. 584)

4. What effect did improved food storage have on population growth?

Refrigerators helped prevent the growth of harmful bacteria, and refrigerated railcars safely transported foods. These developments helped make a balanced diet available year-round. (p. 588)

5. How did the work of the postimpressionist sculptors and painters step away from realism?

By moving away from recognizable realistic scenes (p. 597)

REVIEWING THEMES

1. Citizenship How did education change during the 1800s?

Industrialists and military leaders wanted educated workers and soldiers. Laws were passed in 1870 making public education mandatory, and taxes were levied to support schools. (p. 589)

2. Science, Technology, and Society How did electricity affect communication?

It made it possible to transmit the voice over the wire and text messages over the airwaves. (p. 574)

3. Culture How was romanticism a response to industrialized society?

Reacting against the reason and science of the Industrial Age, the work of the romantics appealed to the imagination and spirit of individuality. These artists were interested in showing life as they thought it should be, not as it really was. (p. 592)

THINKING CRITICALLY

1. Drawing Inferences How did the public education systems that developed in France and the United States help to fulfill the ideas of equality and a representative government?

Education made people more able to participate in government. (p. 589)

2. Making Predictions How might innovations in transportation and communication affect social mobility?

People were able to move into suburbs and commute to work, and information could be shared rapidly over distances. (pp. 588 and 574)

WRITING ABOUT HISTORY

Imagining Imagine that you were born before the invention of the telephone. Write a paragraph describing how you might have communicated with friends and family.

Answers will vary.

STUDY TIPS

1. Have students make a chart comparing how the educational system prior to 1870 and after 1870 affected women and children.

2. Ask students to write a brief paragraph describing how the development of antisepsis by Joseph Lister made surgery safer.

CHAPTER 24

Modern Chapter 15

Chapter Tutorial
The Age of Reform

IDENTIFYING TERMS Choose the term or name that correctly matches each definition.

_____ **1.** the right to vote

_____ **2.** competition among a country's regions

_____ **3.** those who oppose all government

_____ **4.** large, self-sufficient farms

_____ **5.** original inhabitants of New Zealand

a. sectionalism

b. haciendas

c. Maori

d. suffrage

e. anarchists

UNDERSTANDING MAIN IDEAS

1. How did European settlement change the lifestyles of the original inhabitants of New Zealand and Australia?

_____

_____

2. What factors led to the U.S. Civil War?

_____

_____

3. In what ways were the French republicans and monarchists different?

_____

_____

4. What benefits and what problems resulted from the independence movement in Latin America?

_____

_____

5. How were roles determined for colonial women in Latin America?

_____

_____

Chapter 24 Tutorial, continued

REVIEWING THEMES

1. Citizenship How did the reform movement in Britain and the anti-slavery movement in the United States influence women's suffrage?

_____

_____

2. Government How did the Creoles in Latin America respond when Spain tried to regain control of its colonies there?

_____

_____

3. Constitutional Heritage How did most workers in France want the government to be structured?

_____

_____

THINKING CRITICALLY

1. Decision Making Should the French people have voted for Louis-Napoléon? Why do you think they did?

_____

_____

2. Sequencing What major territories were gained by the United States during the 1800s, and in what order were they obtained?

_____

_____

WRITING ABOUT HISTORY

Persuading Imagine you are a woman in Britain in the 1800s. Write a brief speech to the House of Lords explaining why you feel women should have the right to vote.

_____

_____

IDENTIFYING TERMS Choose the term or name that correctly matches each definition.

_d (p. 602)_ **1.** the right to vote

a. sectionalism

_a (p. 611)_ **2.** competition among a country's regions

b. haciendas

_e (p. 619)_ **3.** those who oppose all government

c. Maori

_b (p. 621)_ **4.** large, self-sufficient farms

d. suffrage

_c (p. 608)_ **5.** original inhabitants of New Zealand

e. anarchists

UNDERSTANDING MAIN IDEAS

1. How did European settlement change the lifestyles of the original inhabitants of Australia and New Zealand?

The aboriginals lost their land to immigrants. Many of them died as a result of diseases brought over by the European settlers. (p. 608)

2. What factors led to the U.S. Civil War?

Sectional differences, President Lincoln's election, and the dispute over slavery (p. 611)

3. In what ways were the French republicans and monarchists different?

Republicans believed France should become a republic, grant political rights, and make reforms. Monarchists wanted a direct descendant of King Charles X to be king. (p. 616)

4. What benefits and what problems resulted from the independence movement in Latin America?

Benefits included expanded trade and social reform. The problems included class conflict, civil unrest, and caudillo dictatorships. (pp. 622–627)

5. How were roles determined for colonial women in Latin America?

Rights were determined by ethnic or family background. The small segment of Spanish women enjoyed the most rights because they could own property. (p. 622)

REVIEWING THEMES

1. Citizenship How did the reform movement in Britain and the anti-slavery movement in the United States influence women's suffrage?

The rights of men to vote and abolitionism encouraged suffragettes in both countries to seek the right to vote. (pp. 606 and 614)

2. Government How did the Creoles in Latin America respond when Spain tried to regain control of its colonies there?

They resisted their loss of power and began to call for independence. (pp. 622–625)

3. Constitutional Heritage How did most workers in France want the government to be structured?

They wanted a republic with democracy. (p. 616)

THINKING CRITICALLY

1. Decision Making Should the French people have voted for Louis-Napoléon? Why do you think they did?

Student's opinions will vary. (pp. 616–617)

2. Sequencing What major territories were gained by the United States during the 1800s, and in what order were they obtained?

Louisiana Purchase, Florida Cession, Texas Annexation, Oregon Territory, Mexican Cession, Gadsden Purchase, Alaska, and Hawaii (p. 610)

WRITING ABOUT HISTORY

Persuading Imagine you are a woman in Britain in the 1800s. Write a brief speech to the House of Lords explaining why you feel that women should have the right to vote.

Student essays will vary. (pp. 605–606)

STUDY TIPS

1. Have students write a brief essay agreeing or disagreeing that there should be no restrictions on who may vote in a society.

2. Ask students the Read to Discover questions listed at the beginning of each section. If the students have trouble recalling them, help them find corresponding portions of the text and reread them.

CHAPTER 25

Modern Chapter **16**

Chapter Tutorial

Nationalism in Europe

IDENTIFYING TERMS Choose the term or name that correctly matches each definition.

_____ **1.** ended the Seven Weeks' War   **a.** risorgimento

_____ **2.** resurgence   **b.** Treaty of Prague

_____ **3.** anti-Jewish riots   **c.** Kulturkampf

_____ **4.** gave self-rule to Bulgaria   **d.** pogroms

_____ **5.** anti-Catholic program   **e.** Treaty of San Stefano

UNDERSTANDING MAIN IDEAS

1. What were some of the problems Italy faced after unification?

_____

_____

2. What changes in German government occurred as a result of unification?

_____

_____

3. What factors led to Bismarck's decline in power and his subsequent resignation?

_____

_____

4. How did the Russian government deal with reform movements?

_____

_____

5. Why were the early 1900s filled with tension in Europe?

_____

_____

Chapter 25 Tutorial, *continued*

REVIEWING THEMES

1. Government How did differences in the goals of different political groups affect the unification movements?

_____

_____

2. Global Relations To what extent did threats from other countries influence unification movements?

_____

_____

3. Culture In what countries did common cultural backgrounds play a role in unification?

_____

_____

THINKING CRITICALLY

1. Summarizing Explain how liberalism affected Russia's domestic policy.

_____

_____

2. Drawing Inferences Why did Western nations fear Russian influences in the Balkans?

_____

_____

WRITING ABOUT HISTORY

Opinion Write a paragraph that presents an argument for or against using repression to silence protests.

_____

_____

_____

IDENTIFYING TERMS Choose the term or name that correctly matches each definition.

_b (p. 640)_ **1.** ended the Seven Weeks' War

_a (p. 632)_ **2.** resurgence

_d (p. 651)_ **3.** anti-Jewish riots

_e (p. 656)_ **4.** gave self-rule to Bulgaria

_c (p. 643)_ **5.** anti-Catholic program

a. risorgimento

b. Treaty of Prague

c. Kulturkampf

d. pogroms

e. Treaty of San Stefano

UNDERSTANDING MAIN IDEAS

1. What were some of the problems Italy faced after unification?

Few Italians had experience with self-government; regions of the country remained divided by cultural differences; tensions grew between the industrialized north and the agricultural south. The standard of living of most Italians was low, and labor problems arose. (p. 636)

2. What changes in German government occurred as a result of unification?

King William I was declared emperor. Bismarck accepted a constitution; the federal government controlled national defense, foreign affairs, and commerce. (p. 641)

3. What factors led to Bismarck's decline in power and his subsequent resignation?

William II held strong conservative opinions and felt that Bismarck held too much power. In 1890, when the socialists won huge gains in the elections Bismarck wanted to come up with a new constitution, but William II knew it would be bad for his reign. When Bismarck threatened to resign this time, William II accepted. (p. 646)

4. How did the Russian government deal with reform movements?

Although Alexander II accepted some reform, such as the abolition of serfdom, Alexander III and Nicolas II dealt with reform movements by using censorship, spies, informers, imprisonment, and exile. They also took control of the education system and churches, discriminated against minorities, and intensified Russification. Jews were massacred in pogroms. (p. 651)

5. Why were the early 1900s filled with tension in Europe?

Because of external wars to extend borders for resources, ports, and political power and internal struggles for individual rights (pp. 653–657)

REVIEWING THEMES

1. Government How did differences in the goals of different political groups affect the unification movements?

Differing goals caused internal discord, thus slowing unification. (pp. 632–657)

2. Global Relations To what extent did threats from other countries influence unification movements?

Threats from outside served to unify the populace against the threat. (pp. 632–657)

3. Culture In what countries did common cultural backgrounds play a role in unification?

Italy, Germany, and Russia (pp. 632–652)

THINKING CRITICALLY

1. Summarizing Explain how liberalism affected Russia's domestic policy.

Liberalism led to some concessions in the policies of Alexander II regarding serfs, laborers, and soldiers, but brought brutal repression from later czars.
(pp. 649–652)

2. Drawing Inferences Why did Western nations fear Russian influences in the Balkans?

Great Britain did not want Russia to gain a water route from the Black Sea to the Mediterranean. (p. 655)

WRITING ABOUT HISTORY

Opinion Write a paragraph that presents an argument for or against using repression to silence protests.

Student answers will vary. (p. 652)

STUDY TIPS

1. Have students make a chart comparing the reforms of Alexander II and the policies of Alexander III and Nicolas II.

2. Ask students to write a paragraph describing how they might have felt had they been the victims of a pogrom.

CHAPTER  26

Modern Chapter **17**

Chapter Tutorial

The Age of Imperialism

IDENTIFYING TERMS Choose the term or name that correctly matches each definition.

_____ **1.** when one country takes control of another
_____ **2.** the expected one
_____ **3.** South African War
_____ **4.** the two-house assembly of Japan
_____ **5.** restricted Cuban land transfers

a. al Mahdī
b. Diet
c. Platt Amendment
d. imperialism
e. Boer War

UNDERSTANDING MAIN IDEAS

1. Why were coaling stations important to the imperialists?

_____

_____

2. What role did the al Mahdī play in the history of the Sudan?

_____

_____

3. What role did Cecil Rhodes play in South Africa?

_____

_____

4. What did the Japanese do to industrialize their country?

_____

_____

5. What were some of the main issues of Mexico's civil war?

_____

_____

(Chapter 26 Tutorial, continued)

REVIEWING THEMES

1. Global Relations What evidence exists that an industrialized country can control a country that is not industrialized?

_____

_____

2. Geography What evidence exists to show that areas were colonized because they met the transportation needs of other, more powerful countries?

_____

_____

3. Economics What evidence exists to show that areas were colonized so a more powerful country could obtain their natural resources?

_____

_____

THINKING CRITICALLY

1. Drawing Conclusions Why was colonization probably the most effective means of imperialism?

_____

_____

2. Summarizing Explain the effect of imperialism on sub-Saharan Africa.

_____

_____

WRITING ABOUT HISTORY

Explaining Write a brief paragraph explaining the impact of disease on the building of the Panama Canal.

_____

_____

_____

_____

CHAPTER 26

IDENTIFYING TERMS Choose the term or name that correctly matches each definition.

_d (p. 662)_ **1.** when one country takes control of another   **a.** al Mahdī

_a (p. 669)_ **2.** the expected one   **b.** Diet

_e (p. 673)_ **3.** South African War   **c.** Platt Amendment

_b (p. 676)_ **4.** the two-house assembly of Japan   **d.** imperialism

_c (p. 683)_ **5.** restricted Cuban land transfers   **e.** Boer War

UNDERSTANDING MAIN IDEAS

1. Why were coaling stations important to the imperialists?

They had large navies that needed coal to fuel their ships. During this time, steam-powered boats burned coal. The distance a steamship could travel was from coal station to coal station; small coaling stations on islands were very important strategically. Controlling these islands often was the object of fierce competition between rival naval powers. (p. 663)

2. What role did the al Mahdī play in the history of the Sudan?

The al-Mahdi led a revolt against Egyptian rule in the Sudan. Mahdi's followers gained control of several major Sudanese cities, including the capital. The British acted to stop the Mahdists and prevent the French from gaining control in the Sudan. The Sudan remained under the control of Britain and Egypt. (p. 669)

3. What role did Cecil Rhodes play in South Africa?

He led the British move inland into South Africa, and he took control of the diamond fields in the Boer-controlled Orange Free State. Within 20 years of his arrival, Rhodes completely controlled South African diamond production. Later he organized a colony further north known as Rhodesia, now Zimbabwe. (p. 673)

4. What did the Japanese do to industrialize their country?

They linked cities by telephone and rail and created export goods. This enabled the Japanese to import raw materials they needed, such as iron ore and oil. (p. 677)

5. What were some of the main issues of Mexico's civil war?

The important part of the struggle was over land control. Mexican peasants wanted their land returned to them. (p. 686)

REVIEWING THEMES

1. Global Relations What evidence exists that an industrialized country can control a country that is not industrialized?

Europe, Japan, and the United States controlled many countries that were not industrialized (pp. 662–687)

2. Geography What evidence exists to show that areas were colonized because they met the transportation needs of other, more powerful countries?

British control of the Suez Canal and U.S. control of the Panama Canal. (pp. 668 and 684)

3. Economics What evidence exists to show that areas were colonized so a more powerful country could obtain their natural resources?

King Leopold's rule of the Congo and Rhodes' control of South African diamond production (pp. 670–673)

THINKING CRITICALLY

1. Drawing Conclusions Why was colonization probably the most effective means of imperialism?

Students might say that large groups of colonists living in a conquered land can strongly influence the people and traditions of the "host" country, resulting in a more lasting and dramatic control.

2. Summarizing Explain the effect of imperialism on sub-Saharan Africa.

Despite some benefits (improved medicine, transportation, and agriculture), Africans did not accept European culture and continued to maintain their own identity. The Europeans did not think that the Africans deserved to be treated equally. For the most part, Africans continued to live as they had for centuries. Nearly everything the Europeans did in Africa was for their own benefit. (pp. 673–674)

WRITING ABOUT HISTORY

Explaining Write a brief paragraph explaining the impact of disease on the building of the Panama Canal.

Yellow fever killed many workers attempting to build the canal. By destroying the mosquitoes that carried yellow fever, scientists controlled the spread of the disease. (p. 684)

STUDY TIPS

1. Have students pretend that they are Sultan Moulay Abd al-Hafid. Ask them to write a letter to the French government appealing for aid in restoring order to Morocco. Ask them to state their cause and explain their decision to ask for aid.

2. Ask students to draw a political cartoon dramatizing U.S. imperialism and the implication that the United States has the ability to take whatever it wants from other countries.

CHAPTER  27

Modern Chapter **18**

Chapter Tutorial

World War I and the Russian Revolution

IDENTIFYING TERMS Choose the term or name that correctly matches each definition.

_____ **1.** brutal acts against defenseless civilians   **a.** militarism

_____ **2.** communist forces   **b.** atrocities

_____ **3.** glorification of armed strength   **c.** Red Army

_____ **4.** systematic extermination   **d.** armistice

_____ **5.** agreement to stop fighting   **e.** genocide

UNDERSTANDING MAIN IDEAS

1. What event exploded the Balkan "powder keg" and began World War I?

_____

_____

2. What led the United States to declare war?

_____

_____

3. How did signing the Treaty of Brest Litovsk help the Communist regime in Russia?

_____

_____

4. What problems did the peacemakers at the Paris Peace Conference try to solve?

_____

_____

5. What were the two main goals of the League of Nations?

_____

_____

REVIEWING THEMES

1. Government What role did propaganda play in World War I?

_____

_____

2. Global Relations How did World War I affect relations between the world's greatest powers?

_____

_____

3. Economy How was industry affected by World War I?

_____

_____

THINKING CRITICALLY

1. Drawing Conclusions What were the restrictions on Germany in the Treaty of Versailles, and why were they largely ineffective?

_____

_____

2. Identifying Cause and Effect What effect might the March 1917 revolution in Russia have had on the decision of the United States to join the war?

_____

_____

WRITING ABOUT HISTORY

Point of View Write a brief paragraph explaining what the socialists believed.

_____

_____

_____

_____

Chapter Tutorial

IDENTIFYING TERMS Choose the term or name that correctly matches each definition.

_b (p. 710)_ **1.** brutal acts against defenseless civilians

_c (p. 713)_ **2.** communist forces

_a (p. 698)_ **3.** glorification of armed strength

_e (p. 721)_ **4.** systematic extermination

_d (p. 715)_ **5.** agreement to stop fighting

a. militarism

b. atrocities

c. Red Army

d. armistice

e. genocide

UNDERSTANDING MAIN IDEAS

1. What event exploded the Balkan "powder keg" and began World War I?

The assassination of Archduke Francis Ferdinand and his wife by a Serbian nationalist (p. 701)

2. What led the United States to declare war?

German foreign minister Zimmermann sent a telegram to the Mexican government proposing an alliance between them. Germany offered to help Mexico regain Arizona, New Mexico, and Texas if it would fight on Germany's side. The British intercepted the telegram, and the Americans were outraged at Germany's proposal. Americans also died in U-boat attacks. The Russian revolutionaries overthrew the czarist government, gaining support from Americans who wanted to spread democracy. (p. 710)

3. How did signing the Treaty of Brest Litovsk help the Communist regime in Russia?

They were able to turn their attention to internal political matters. (p. 713)

4. What problems did the peacemakers at the Paris Peace Conference try to solve?

They tried to make a treaty that was fair to all and settle conflicting territorial demands. They decided questions of reparations and created a world organization to maintain peace called the League of Nations. (p. 716)

5. What were the two main goals of the League of Nations?

To promote international cooperation and to keep peace among nations by settling disputes and reducing armaments (p. 722)

REVIEWING THEMES

1. Government What role did propaganda play in World War I?

Governments used selected bits of information, both true and false, to get people to back their countries' war efforts. (p. 706)

2. **Global Relations** How did World War I affect relations between the world's greatest powers?

The Treaty of Versailles and the League of Nations helped form strong alliances among Western powers. German resentment of the peace settlement, however, led to World War II. (p. 722)

3. **Economy** How was industry affected by World War I?

There were many new inventions, and production was increased to meet the demands of the war effort. (pp. 705–706)

THINKING CRITICALLY

1. **Drawing Conclusions** What were the restrictions on Germany in the Treaty of Versailles, and why were they largely ineffective?

Germany had to abolish its military draft and keep an army of only 100,000 men. Germany was not allowed to manufacture heavy artillery, tanks, or military airplanes. The German Navy could have a few warships, but no submarines. The Allies lacked the ability to enforce these rules. (pp. 718–719)

2. **Identifying Cause and Effect** What effect might the March 1917 revolution in Russia have had on the decision of the United States to join the war?

Americans favored any group that was fighting for democracy. (p. 710)

WRITING ABOUT HISTORY

Point of View Write a brief paragraph explaining what the socialists believed.

Answers may vary, but students should include the concept that politcal equality must be coupled with economic equality. (p. 711)

STUDY TIPS

1. Have students create a cause-and-effect chart that shows the events that ended Russia's participation in World War I.

2. Ask students to write a brief paragraph explaining why the Balkans were considered a "powder keg."

Modern Chapter **19**

Chapter Tutorial

The Great Depression and the Rise of Totalitarianism

IDENTIFYING TERMS Choose the term or name that correctly matches each definition.

_____ 1. brings the conscious and unconscious together

_____ 2. provided unemployment and old age benefits

_____ 3. Irish nationalist party

_____ 4. from the Latin word *fasces*

_____ 5. government-controlled economics

a. Social Security Act

b. surrealism

c. command economy

d. Sinn Fein

e. fascism

UNDERSTANDING MAIN IDEAS

1. How did Freud's notion of the irrational and the subconscious influence postwar literature?

_____

_____

2. What New Deal programs led to reforms in the American economy?

_____

_____

3. What economic and political problems did France face after World War I?

_____

_____

4. How did Hitler turn Germany into a police state after 1933?

_____

_____

5. How did Stalin ensure loyalty from government and party officials and from the Soviet people?

_____

_____

Chapter 28 Tutorial, continued

REVIEWING THEMES

1. Global Relations Why did western European nations and the United States fail to respond to Germany's violations of the Treaty of Versailles?

_____

_____

2. Government How did Hitler use Germany's democratic system to gain control of the country?

_____

_____

3. Culture How did the work of Freud and Einstein influence culture during the 1920s?

_____

_____

THINKING CRITICALLY

1. Finding the Main Idea What was life like for the average Soviet citizen during the 1930s?

_____

_____

2. Supporting a Point of View Explain how postwar literature reflected a new era.

_____

_____

WRITING ABOUT HISTORY

Finding the Cause What were some signs that postwar prosperity was crumbling?

_____

_____

_____

CHAPTER 28

The Great Depression and the Rise of Totalitarianism

IDENTIFYING TERMS Choose the term or name that correctly matches each definition.

<u>b (p. 730)</u> **1.** brings the conscious and unconscious together

<u>a (p. 737)</u> **2.** provided unemployment and old age benefits

<u>d (p. 741)</u> **3.** Irish nationalist party

<u>e (p. 743)</u> **4.** from the Latin word *fasces*

<u>c (p. 750)</u> **5.** government-controlled economics

a. Social Security Act

b. surrealism

c. command economy

d. Sinn Fein

e. fascism

UNDERSTANDING MAIN IDEAS

1. How did Freud's notion of the irrational and the subconscious influence postwar literature?

Writers used Freud's ideas to help them understand and write about the dreadful destruction of the war and the uneasiness that people around the world continued to experience. (p. 729)

2. What New Deal programs led to reforms in the American economy?

The program created jobs by hiring people to construct public buildings, roads, and other projects. It also led to the Social Security Act of 1935, which provided unemployment and old-age benefits. (p. 737)

3. What economic and political problems did France face after World War I?

High prices hurt industrial workers and the lower middle class. Government expenses rose, and payments had to be made to French citizens and the United States for war materials. Additionally, interest payments on the national debt further decreased the treasury. (p. 738)

4. How did Hitler turn Germany into a police state after 1933?

Someone set fire to the Reichstag building. Hitler blamed the Communists and received emergency powers to deal with the supposed Communist revolt. He used these powers to make himself dictator. (p. 746)

5. How did Stalin ensure loyalty from government and party officials and from the Soviet people?

By using informers and secret police (p. 751)

REVIEWING THEMES

1. Global Relations Why did western European nations and the United States fail to respond to Germany's violations of the Treaty of Versailles?

In the 1930s, Germany began secretly rebuilding its military. In early 1936, Hitler ordered troops into the Rhineland. This violated the Treaty of Versailles. Neither France nor Great Britian reacted to this treaty violation because neither of them believed that the violation was worth going to war over. (p. 748)

2. **Government** How did Hitler use Germany's democratic system to gain control of the country?

In 1932, the Nazi Party won 230 seats in the Reichstag, one house of the German parliament. By 1932, the Nazis held more seats than any other party. (p. 746)

3. **Culture** How did the work of Freud and Einstein influence culture during the 1920s?

Freud's theories helped people understand irrational events of life and war, and Einstein's argument that all things were relative helped people understand that values differ, and that no one could say that one set of principles was good for all groups. (pp. 728–729)

THINKING CRITICALLY

1. **Finding the Main Idea** What was life like for the average Soviet citizen during the 1930s?

Financially difficult and personally dangerous (pp. 751–753)

2. **Supporting a Point of View** Explain how postwar literature reflected a new era.

It reflected dissatisfaction with traditional ideas, tried to offer a new vision, and experimented with form. (pp. 729–730)

WRITING ABOUT HISTORY

Finding the Cause What were some signs that postwar prosperity was crumbling?

Farmers were suffering because croplands had been destroyed during the war; trade limitations and high tariffs were driving Europeans into debt because they could not purchase goods; and the U.S. stock market fell, forcing many people into debt. (pp. 734–735)

STUDY TIPS

1. Have students write a paragraph describing the purpose of the gulag, and how life was for the prisoners. Ask students to include the reasons Russian citizens might find themselves in the gulag.

2. Ask students to make a time line of events in Great Britain after the war, including the rise of the Irish independence movement.

Chapter Tutorial

Modern Chapter **20**

Nationalist Movements Around the World

IDENTIFYING TERMS Choose the term or name that correctly matches each definition.

_____ **1.** aimed to build a Palestinian homeland for Jews

_____ **2.** leader of the Indian nationalist movement

_____ **3.** all nations have equal rights to trade in China

_____ **4.** ended the Russo-Japanese War

_____ **5.** Cuban army sergeant

a. Open Door policy

b. Mohandas Gandhi

c. Treaty of Portsmouth

d. Fulgencio Batista

e. Zionism

UNDERSTANDING MAIN IDEAS

1. What were the policies of passive resistance?

_____

_____

2. Why did Mustafa Kemal feel it was necessary to separate the government from Islam in order to carry out his programs?

_____

_____

3. What crucial problems did the Nationalists government of Chiang Kai-shek fail to deal with?

_____

_____

4. How did Japan position itself to be an important power during the early 1900s?

_____

_____

5. How did the Great Depression affect Latin America?

_____

_____

_____

Chapter 29 Tutorial, continued

REVIEWING THEMES

1. Government How did the military affect Japan's government?

_____

_____

2. Culture How did cultural issues influence nationalistic movements in Africa?

_____

_____

3. Economics How did economic issues influence political events in Latin America?

_____

_____

THINKING CRITICALLY

1. Evaluating How would you evaluate Mustafa Kemal's attempt to modernize Turkey?

_____

_____

2. Reasoning What event led Mohandas Gandhi to lead a revolt against British rule, and why was he revered as a spiritual leader?

_____

_____

WRITING ABOUT HISTORY

Persuading What were the main causes for the rise of economic nationalism in Latin America?

_____

_____

_____

_____

Chapter Tutorial

Nationalist Movements Around the World

IDENTIFYING TERMS Choose the term or name that correctly matches each definition.

_e (p. 760)_ **1.** aimed to build a Palestinian homeland for Jews

_b (p. 760)_ **2.** leader of the Indian nationalist movement

_a (p. 765)_ **3.** all nations have equal rights to trade in China

_c (p. 771)_ **4.** ended the Russo-Japanese War

_d (p. 776)_ **5.** Cuban army sergeant

a. Open Door policy

b. Mohandas Gandhi

c. Treaty of Portsmouth

d. Fulgencio Batista

e. Zionism

UNDERSTANDING MAIN IDEAS

1. What were the policies of passive resistance?

Passive resistance included boycotting British goods, refusing to pay taxes, and nonviolent protest. (pp. 760–761)

2. Why did Mustafa Kemal feel it was necessary to separate the government from Islam in order to carry out his programs?

He believed that Islam was a roadblock to modernization. (p. 762)

3. What crucial problems did the Nationalist government of Chiang Kai-shek fail to deal with?

They did not change the oppressive system of land ownership because they wanted the support of the landowners and merchants. They also failed to change tax collection methods. (p. 768)

4. How did Japan position itself to be an important power during the early 1900s?

They destroyed the Russian Baltic fleet and obtained favorable terms in the Treaty of Portsmouth. (p. 771)

5. How did the Great Depression affect Latin America?

Because they received little for their exports, many Latin American nations found it impossible to import anything but the most essential goods, and some countries stopped paying their foreign debts. (p. 775)

REVIEWING THEMES

1. Government How did the military affect Japan's government?

Military needs, values, and goals shape a nation's civil lifestyle and its domestic and international policies. (p. 772)

2. Culture How did cultural issues influence nationalistic movements in Africa?

The war broadened Africans' experiences, and they brought home with them new ideas about freedom and nationalism. Colonial education taught them about freedom and racism, and political repression made many Africans seek independence. (p. 764)

3. Economics How did economic issues influence political events in Latin America?

Coups d'état overthrew constitutional governments, and the middle class rebelled. (p. 750)

THINKING CRITICALLY

1. Evaluating How would you evaluate Mustafa Kemal's attempt to modernize Turkey?

Students may note that Turkey became independent and prosperous. (p. 762)

2. Reasoning What event led Mohandas Gandhi to lead a revolt against British rule, and why was he revered as a spiritual leader?

A massacre of Hindus by British authorities convinced Gandhi that India must strive for complete independence. His humble manner and attire inspired millions and earned him great respect. His followers called him Mahatma, or "Great Soul." (p. 760)

WRITING ABOUT HISTORY

Persuading What were the main causes for the rise of economic nationalism in Latin America?

With the global depression, international markets for Latin American goods were weak and imported goods were costly. Countries had no choice but to develop their own industries to manufacture goods. This economic nationalism joined with growing feelings of political nationalism. The middle class in particular no longer wanted to be dependent on the United States or Europe. (p. 777)

STUDY TIPS

1. Have students write a short story imaging that they are the Emperor Pu Yi, the last emperor of China. Ask them to describe how it might have felt to go from privilege to imprisonment.

2. Ask students to write a brief paragraph describing the cause and effects of the Boxer Rebellion and the influence of the Empress Dowager Tz'u-hsi.

Chapter Tutorial

CHAPTER 30

Modern Chapter **21**

World War II

IDENTIFYING TERMS Choose the term or name that correctly matches each definition.

_____ **1.** an agreement making war illegal

_____ **2.** September 1938 meeting called by Hitler

_____ **3.** "lightning war"

_____ **4.** people willing to help their country's enemies

_____ **5.** Nazi genocide

a. blitzkrieg

b. Holocaust

c. Kellogg-Briand Pact

d. Munich Conference

e. collaborators

UNDERSTANDING MAIN IDEAS

1. Why did Japan feel its aggression would not be opposed by the League of Nations?

_____

_____

2. According to Lindbergh, in what sense would democracy have failed if the United States went to war?

_____

_____

3. What role did the French Resistance play in undermining the Nazi war effort?

_____

_____

4. What was Germany's plan to gain control of the Soviet Union, and how successful was the Soviet Union's defense?

_____

_____

5. How was the Final Solution an extension of Nazi philosophy?

_____

_____

6. How did the Allies win the war with Japan?

_____

Chapter 30 Tutorial, continued

REVIEWING THEMES

1. Global Relations How did the 1939 Revised Neutrality Act of the United States aid the international war effort?

_____

_____

2. Government How did the United States respond to Japanese aggression in Indochina?

_____

_____

3. Science and Technology How was the technology of World War II both beneficial and destructive?

_____

_____

THINKING CRITICALLY

1. Making Generalizations How did American use of the atomic bomb affect the aftermath of World War II?

_____

_____

2. Summarizing What violations of human rights took place during World War II?

_____

_____

WRITING ABOUT HISTORY

Viewpoint What has *The Diary of Anne Frank* come to represent?

_____

_____

_____

_____

IDENTIFYING TERMS Choose the term or name that correctly matches each definition.

_c (p. 782)_ **1.** an agreement making war illegal

_d (p. 787)_ **2.** September 1938 meeting called by Hitler

_a (p. 791)_ **3.** "lightning war"

_e (p. 791)_ **4.** people willing to help their country's enemies

_b (p. 803)_ **5.** Nazi genocide

a. blitzkrieg

b. Holocaust

c. Kellogg-Briand Pact

d. Munich Conference

e. collaborators

UNDERSTANDING MAIN IDEAS

1. Why did Japan feel its aggression would not be opposed by the League of Nations?

Although the League of Nations condemned Japan's aggression against China, they were not willing to retaliate. This lack of opposition encouraged Japan, which then announced its intention to extend its influence throughout East Asia and the Western Pacific. (p. 782)

2. According to Lindbergh, in what sense would democracy have failed if the United States went to war?

He felt that war was against the wishes of the majority, and that would be a violation of the principles of democracy. (p. 787)

3. What role did the French Resistance play in undermining the Nazi war effort?

They undermined the Nazi war effort by engaging in acts of sabotage such as blowing up bridges, wrecking trains, and cutting telephone and telegraph lines. (p. 793)

4. What was Germany's plan to gain control of the Soviet Union, and how successful was the Soviet Union's defense?

Germany invaded the Soviet Union, and opened up a new front in the east. The Soviets resorted to a scorched earth defense, and as a result, Germany had to stay longer than expected through the bitter Russian winter. When the Russians launched a winter counter attack, the Germans retreated. (p. 798)

5. How was the Final Solution an extension of Nazi philosophy?

Hitler believed a pure "Aryan race" would colonize conquered areas; eliminating non-Aryans made it possible to take over their land. (p. 801)

6. How did the Allies win the war with Japan?

Through the use of atomic bombs on Nagasaki and Hiroshima. (p. 808)

REVIEWING THEMES

1. Global Relations How did the 1939 Revised Neutrality Act of the United States aid the international war effort?

It allowed American firms to sell munitions to warring nations on a cash-and-carry basis. The real effect of this law was to allow the sale of arms only to Great Britain. (p. 794)

2. Government How did the United States respond to Japanese aggression in Indochina?

The United States responded in three ways: (1) It protested the violations of the Nine-Power Pact of 1922. (2) It provided assistance to Chinese Nationalists and placed an embargo on the sale of oil and scrap iron to Japan. (3) It moved a large part of its Pacific Fleet to Hawaii. (p. 799)

3. Science and Technology How was the technology of World War II both beneficial and destructive?

Airplanes and bombs did great damage; however, radar saved lives by forewarning of enemy planes and attack. (p. 794)

THINKING CRITICALLY

1. Making Generalizations How did American use of the atomic bomb affect the aftermath of World War II?

American use of nuclear weapons ushered in the atomic age, and with it many new questions and fears. (p. 809)

2. Summarizing What violations of human rights took place during World War II?

Jews, Slavs, Gypsies, and others were murdered by Nazis during the Holocaust. Victims in concentration camps suffered forced labor, starvation, brutality, filth, and disease. (p. 803)

WRITING ABOUT HISTORY

Viewpoint What has *The Diary of Anne Frank* come to represent?

The horrors of the Holocaust (p. 803)

STUDY TIPS

1. Ask students to imagine that they are Anne Frank. Have them write a journal entry describing how it might have felt to remain in hiding for such a long time.

2. Have students draw a time line that shows the progression of American entry into World War II.

Name _____ Class _____ Date _____

IDENTIFYING TERMS Choose the term or name that correctly matches each definition.

_____ **1.** the power to defeat a measure with a single vote   **a.** Warsaw Pact

_____ **2.** a 20-year mutual defense agreement   **b.** Nikita Khrushchev

_____ **3.** commitment to restrict communism   **c.** welfare state

_____ **4.** government is responsible for social well-being   **d.** veto power

_____ **5.** Stalin's successor   **e.** containment

UNDERSTANDING MAIN IDEAS

1. How did territorial adjustments affect the German economy?

_____

_____

2. What were the cause and effect of the Berlin blockade?

_____

_____

3. What was the West German miracle and what produced it?

_____

_____

4. Why did the United States become involved in the conflict in Vietnam?

_____

_____

5. How did the American civil rights movement affect the world?

_____

_____

REVIEWING THEMES

1. Economics Briefly descibe the economy of the postwar United States.

_____

_____

2. Government What problems regarding democracy did the separatist movement in Canada raise?

_____

_____

3. Citizenship What sort of protests did civil rights activists rely on in the 1960s?

_____

_____

THINKING CRITICALLY

1. Identifying Cause and Effect Why did the British economy face continuing difficulties in the postwar era?

_____

_____

2. Drawing Inferences Why did Khrushchev criticize Stalin's rule?

_____

_____

WRITING ABOUT HISTORY

Persuading Write a brief paragraph explaining how Charles de Gaulle's treatment of French territories in Africa might have related to his views about alliances.

_____

_____

_____

IDENTIFYING TERMS Choose the term or name that correctly matches each definition.

d (p. 823) **1.** the power to defeat a measure with a single vote

a (p. 830) **2.** a 20-year mutual defense agreement

e (p. 827) **3.** commitment to restrict communism

c (p. 832) **4.** government is responsible for social well-being

b (p. 835) **5.** Stalin's successor

a. Warsaw Pact

b. Nikita Khrushchev

c. welfare state

d. veto power

e. containment

UNDERSTANDING MAIN IDEAS

1. How did territorial adjustments affect the German economy?

The transfer of parts of Germany to Poland and the Soviet Union stripped Germany of one-fourth of its land. The territorial adjustments also led to a large increase in Germany's population. The burden of feeding, housing, and employing these refugees fell on a shrunken and divided postwar Germany. (p. 822)

2. What were the cause and effect of the Berlin blockade?

The Soviets opposed reunification and imposed a blockade on the border of East Germany to all land and water traffic into Berlin from the west. West Berlin soon faced starvation. (p. 828)

3. What was the West German miracle and what produced it?

Rapid reconstruction and industrial development under free-market policies. (p. 831)

4. Why did the United States become involved in the conflict in Vietnam?

The United States committed ever-increasing numbers of troops to help South Vietnam in its struggle against communist North Vietnam. (p. 840)

5. How did the American civil rights movement affect the world?

It provided the inspiration for similar movements around the world. (p. 838)

REVIEWING THEMES

1. Economics Briefly descibe the economy of the postwar United States.

After World War II, the U.S. economy reached new heights with new industries and the rapid growth of new construction. Although there were several minor recessions, by the 1960s, there was continuous economic growth. (p. 837)

2. Government What problems regarding democracy did the separatist movement in Canada raise?

Canadians were forced to vote on unity, and a slim majority overruled the majority. (p. 841)

3. Citizenship What sort of protests did civil rights activists rely on in the 1960s?

Nonviolent methods such as boycotts, marches, sit-ins, and mass demonstrations (p. 838)

THINKING CRITICALLY

1. Identifying Cause and Effect Why did the British economy face continuing difficulties in the postwar era?

Its industrial equipment was inefficient and outdated. Many workers had died in the war, and some scientists and managers had emigrated to Australia, Canada, or the United States. After the war, Britain lost valuable colonies and possessions, and the cost of its remaining overseas commitments was a heavy burden. (p. 832)

2. Drawing Inferences Why did Khrushchev criticize Stalin's rule?

For crimes committed by Stalin and the restrictions he placed on the Soviet people, along with his state-sponsored terrorism (p. 835)

WRITING ABOUT HISTORY

Persuading Write a brief paragraph explaining how Charles de Gaulle's treatment of French territories in Africa might have related to his views about alliances.

Students' responses will vary; however, they might mention that he granted independence to 12 French territories in Africa. (p. 833)

STUDY TIPS

1. Have students make a diagram describing the types of war crimes of the WWII era.

2. Ask students to make a chart listing the six main bodies of the United Nations and their functions.

 **Chapter Tutorial**

Modern Chapter **23**   **Asia Since 1945**

IDENTIFYING TERMS Choose the term or name that correctly matches each definition.

_____ **1.** South Korea, Taiwan, Singapore, Hong Kong   **a.** Aung San Suu Kyi

_____ **2.** won Nobel Peace Prize   **b.** Great Leap Forward

_____ **3.** Mao Zedong's five-year plan   **c.** Deng Xiaoping

_____ **4.** leader of Chinese moderates   **d.** Dalai Lama

_____ **5.** Tibet's Buddhist religious leader   **e.** Four Tigers

UNDERSTANDING MAIN IDEAS

1. What problems did Pakistan face after it became independent?

_____

_____

2. How did life in China differ after Mao Zedong's death from what it had been before?

_____

_____

3. What steps did Japan take to become a major world economic power?

_____

_____

4. What were the results of strong government control in the Philippines and Indonesia?

_____

_____

5. How did Asia become a region of powerful economic growth?

_____

_____

Chapter 32 Tutorial, continued

REVIEWING THEMES

1. **Government** What evidence exists that people had fewer civil rights in Asian countries that had strong controlling governments?

_____

_____

2. **Global Relations** List examples of clashes between neighboring communist and non-communist Asian nations.

_____

_____

3. **Economics** What are examples of Asian countries whose income growth has led to outstanding successes?

_____

_____

THINKING CRITICALLY

1. **Summarizing** What problems did the new independent nations of Asia have in common?

_____

_____

2. **Drawing Inferences** How did the World Bank and the International Monetary Fund affect Asian growth?

_____

_____

WRITING ABOUT HISTORY

Persuading Write a brief paragraph explaining the aim of China's Red Guard.

_____

_____

_____

CHAPTER 32

Modern Chapter **23**

IDENTIFYING TERMS Choose the term or name that correctly matches each definition.

_e (p. 872)_ **1.** South Korea, Taiwan, Singapore, Hong Kong

_a (p. 864)_ **2.** won Nobel Peace Prize

_b (p. 853)_ **3.** Mao Zedong's five-year plan

_c (p. 855)_ **4.** leader of Chinese moderates

_d (p. 850)_ **5.** Tibet's Buddhist religious leader

a. Aung San Suu Kyi

b. Great Leap Forward

c. Deng Xiaoping

d. Dalai Lama

e. Four Tigers

UNDERSTANDING MAIN IDEAS

1. What problems did Pakistan face after it became independent?

When British rule ended, Pakistan became a two-part country, East and West Pakistan, separated by India. The two parts of Pakistan had different languages, cultures, and geography. It was almost impossible to govern the two parts as one country. The government soon lost control of the country to military leaders. (p. 850)

2. How did life in China differ after Mao Zedong's death from what it had been before?

China moved towards a market economy and a more open society. It began to allow privately owned businesses. (p. 855)

3. What steps did Japan take to become a major world economic power?

Japan instituted land reform and broke up huge industrial firms controlled by powerful families whose size was preventing free trade. They began to take advantage of a highly skilled work force to produce advanced technology for the world market. (p. 860)

4. What were the results of strong government control in the Philippines and Indonesia?

The economy weakened (pp. 864–866)

5. How did Asia become a region of powerful economic growth?

Economic cooperation between Asian nations and greater government control (p. 872)

REVIEWING THEMES

1. Government What evidence exists that people had fewer civil rights in Asian countries that had strong controlling governments?

The Tiananmen Square Massacre; Aung San Suu Kyi's arrest in Burma; tight controls in Malaysia (pp. 855, 864, and 870)

2. Global Relations List examples of clashes between neighboring communist and non-communist Asian nations.

Korean War, Vietnam War, North Vietnam's intervention in Laos and Cambodia (pp. 856, 867, and 868–869)

3. Economics What are examples of Asian countries whose income growth has led to outstanding successes?

South Korea, Singapore, Japan, Hong Kong, and Taiwan (p. 872)

THINKING CRITICALLY

1. Summarizing What problems did the new independent nations of Asia have in common?

Civil unrest, communist insurgencies, poor economies (pp. 863–869)

2. Drawing Inferences How did the World Bank and the International Monetary Fund affect Asian growth?

They helped by making loans for economic development. (p. 872)

WRITING ABOUT HISTORY

Persuading Write a brief paragraph explaining the aim of China's Red Guard.

Answers may vary; however, students should mention that the goal of the Red Guard was to purify China's political scene by ridding it of opposition to Mao Zedong. They also tried to destroy any symbols of ancient Chinese culture. (p. 854)

STUDY TIPS

1. Have students make a list of the important and influential women of Asia listed in the chapter. Ask students to write a few sentences on the contributions of each to Asian society.

2. Ask students to create a chart to organize details of times when existing governments in Southeast Asia were taken over without consent. Who took over, the reasons, and the results should be included. Countries of Southeast Asia should include the Philippines, Burma, Indonesia, Vietnam, Laos, and Cambodia.

CHAPTER **33**

Modern Chapter **24**

Chapter Tutorial

Africa and the Middle East Since 1945

IDENTIFYING TERMS Choose the term or name that correctly matches each definition.

_____ **1.** secret Kikuyu organization

_____ **2.** segregation and economic exploitation

_____ **3.** a collective farm

_____ **4.** Iranian nationalist leader

_____ **5.** Nigerian playwright and poet

a. apartheid

b. Mau Mau

c. Wole Soyinka

d. kibbutz

e. Mohammad Mosaddeq

UNDERSTANDING MAIN IDEAS

1. How did South Africa's experience of colonialism and independence differ from that of other nations of Africa?

_____

_____

2. What were the causes of ethnic conflicts in Africa, and how might they have been reduced?

_____

_____

3. What was the response of the west to Mosaddeq's nationalization of Iran's oil industry?

_____

_____

4. What was Turkey's response to postwar pressure from the Soviet Union?

_____

_____

5. Why is the Middle East still a source of major concern?

_____

_____

REVIEWING THEMES

1. Government How did the way the people of the Belgian Congo achieved their independence affect their nation?

_____

_____

2. Culture In which countries have the presence of different cultures contributed to unrest and civil war?

_____

_____

3. Economics How have the rich oil fields of the Middle East and North Africa affected the lives of people there?

_____

_____

THINKING CRITICALLY

1. Sequencing Trace the events leading to the rise and fall of apartheid in South Africa.

_____

_____

2. Identifying Cause and Effect What were the causes and results of the Arab-Israeli war of 1948–1949?

_____

_____

WRITING ABOUT HISTORY

Persuading Write a brief paragraph explaining some possible causes of ethnic violence.

_____

_____

_____

Chapter Tutorial

Africa and the Middle East Since 1945

IDENTIFYING TERMS Choose the term or name that correctly matches each definition.

_b (p. 881)_ **1.** secret Kikuyu organization

_a (p. 884)_ **2.** segregation and economic exploitation

_d (p. 893)_ **3.** a collective farm

_e (p. 896)_ **4.** Iranian nationalist leader

_c (p. 890)_ **5.** Nigerian playwright and poet

a. apartheid

b. Mau Mau

c. Wole Soyinka

d. kibbutz

e. Mohammad Mosaddeq

UNDERSTANDING MAIN IDEAS

1. How did South Africa's experience of colonialism and independence differ from that of other nations of Africa?

It was a white-ruled nation with dominion status, linked to Great Britain only in foreign affairs. Internally, it ruled itself as it saw fit. (p. 884)

2. What were the causes of ethnic conflicts in Africa, and how might they have been reduced?

National boundaries had been drawn by imperialist powers for their own convenience. People of similar cultural backgrounds were often separated, while people of different cultures were grouped together. In some places, such as Nigeria, this led to civil war. In order to avoid conflict, the leaders could have been more sensitive to cultural issues. (p. 887)

3. What was the response of the west to Mosaddeq's nationalization of Iran's oil industry?

The British called the nationalization illegal and organized a worldwide boycott of Iranian oil. The U.S. Central Intelligence Agency supported a coup against Mosaddeq and restored power to Mohammad Reza Pahlavi. (p. 896)

4. What was Turkey's response to postwar pressure from the Soviet Union?

Turkish leaders allied themselves more closely with the United States and the Western World. (p. 897)

5. Why is the Middle East still a source of major concern?

The danger of war in the region remains high. (p. 905)

REVIEWING THEMES

1. Government How did the way the people of the Belgian Congo achieved their independence affect their nation?

Independence came so quickly that African leaders were not fully prepared, and a military dictatorship was eventually established. (p. 883)

2. Culture In which countries have the presence of different cultures contributed to unrest and civil war?

Nigeria, Rwanda, Burundi, Zaire (pp. 887–888)

3. Economics How have the rich oil fields of the Middle East and North Africa affected the lives of people there?

It has brought both wealth and power to the regions. (p. 901)

THINKING CRITICALLY

1. Sequencing Trace the events leading to the rise and fall of apartheid in South Africa.

Afrikaans came to power; segregation and economic exploitation became a government policy; protests against apartheid occurred; the government began to retreat from its policies in the 1980s; de Klerk helped end apartheid. (pp. 884–885)

2. Identifying Cause and Effect What were the causes and results of the Arab-Israeli war of 1948–1949?

Causes: Holocaust survivors immigrated to Palestine, Zionist groups waged a terrorist campaign against British authorities, the United Nations voted to partition Palestine, and Arab countries moved against Israel. Effects: Israel won more territory, and many Palestinians became refugees. (pp. 892–893)

WRITING ABOUT HISTORY

Persuading Write a brief paragraph explaining some possible causes of ethnic violence.

Students' answers will vary, but should include the concept of intolerance between people holding different cultural and religious ideas. (pp. 887–888)

STUDY TIPS

1. Have students write a paragraph outlining the cause and effect of the ethnic conflict between the Hutu and Tutsi tribes of Rwanda, Burundi, and Zaire.

2. Ask students to explain and identify the significance of Menachem Begin, Gamal Abel Nasser, and Mohammad Mosaddeq.

Modern Chapter **25**

Chapter Tutorial

Latin America Since 1945

IDENTIFYING TERMS Choose the term or name that correctly matches each definition.

_____ **1.** identify goods and replace them

_____ **2.** political party of Mexico

_____ **3.** Peruvian president

_____ **4.** Argentinian dictator

_____ **5.** leader of Cuban revolution

a. import substitution

b. Juan Perón

c. PRI

d. Alberto Fujimori

e. Fidel Castro

UNDERSTANDING MAIN IDEAS

1. Why were the economies in Latin America so unstable?

_____

_____

2. How did Mexico's economic problems affect emigration?

_____

_____

3. What happened to the Cuban economy when the Soviet Union reduced aid?

_____

_____

4. What role did the military play in Argentina's recent past?

_____

_____

5. What caused the Colombian drug trade to increase, and how did it affect the country?

_____

_____

Chapter 34 Tutorial, continued

REVIEWING THEMES

1. **Economics** How did poor economic conditions affect political events in Latin America?

_____

_____

2. **Government** What methods did Latin American dictators use to retain their control of a country?

_____

_____

3. **Global Relations** Why has the United States sometimes involved itself in Latin American political situations?

_____

_____

THINKING CRITICALLY

1. **Finding the Main Idea** Why did Oscar Arias believe that there would be no peace in Latin America without democracy?

_____

_____

2. **Supporting a Point of View** Why did the United States feel justified in invading Panama?

_____

_____

WRITING ABOUT HISTORY

Persuading Based on what you have learned, write a brief paragraph for or against Puerto Rican statehood.

_____

_____

_____

IDENTIFYING TERMS Choose the term or name that correctly matches each definition.

a (p. 911) **1.** identify goods and replace them

c (p. 915) **2.** political party of Mexico

d (p. 932) **3.** Peruvian president

b (p. 930) **4.** Argentinian dictator

e (p. 922) **5.** leader of Cuban revolution

a. import substitution

b. Juan Perón

c. PRI

d. Alberto Fujimori

e. Fidel Castro

UNDERSTANDING MAIN IDEAS

1. Why were the economies in Latin America so unstable?

Almost every country in the region relied on just one or two crops or minerals for exporting. When world prices rose or fell, the economies of the countries rose or fell. (p. 911)

2. How did Mexico's economic problems affect emigration?

The economy did not grow as fast as the population, and too many people could not find jobs. As a result, thousands of Mexicans began to enter the United States illegally, looking for work. (p. 916)

3. What happened to the Cuban economy when the Soviet Union reduced aid?

With little Soviet aid and a U.S. economic boycott in effect, the Cuban economy nearly collapsed. The government began a rationing program and imposed restrictions on the purchase of consumer goods. (p. 924)

4. What role did the military play in Argentina's recent past?

They controlled the government, engaged in a dirty war, and invaded the Falkland Islands. After their defeat by the British, free elections were held. (p. 931)

5. What caused the Colombian drug trade to increase, and how did it affect the country?

Illegal drug use in the United States and Europe increased, and Colombians realized they could make money growing cocaine and marijuana. Rival drug gangs brought increased violence and crime. (p. 933)

REVIEWING THEMES

1. Economics How did poor economic conditions affect political events in Latin America?

Poor economics led to continued political instability. (pp. 910–914, 921)

2. Government What methods did Latin American dictators use to retain their control of a country?

Suppression of dissent; torture, kidnapping, and often murder (p. 913–914, 919)

3. Global Relations Why has the United States sometimes involved itself in Latin American political situations?

To prevent the spread of communism and to protect its interests in the region (pp. 919–920)

THINKING CRITICALLY

1. Finding the Main Idea Why did Oscar Arias believe that there would be no peace in Latin America without democracy?

He stated that democracy supported peace. He stated that there had never been a single war in Latin America between two democracies. (p. 921)

2. Supporting a Point of View Why did the United States feel justified in invading Panama?

The United States asserted that Panamanian dictator Manuel Noriega was helping South American nations bring drugs into the United States. Panamanian soldiers killed an American soldier and harassed others. President George Bush believed that order needed to be restored. (p. 920)

WRITING ABOUT HISTORY

Persuading Based on what you have learned, write a brief paragraph for or against Puerto Rican statehood.

Answers will vary. (p. 925)

STUDY TIPS

1. Have students write a short essay analyzing why it was a positive move for Violeta Barrios de Chamorro to declare amnesty for many involved in the Nicaraguan civil war.

2. Ask students to write a brief paragraph explaining the North American Free Trade Agreement (NAFTA).

CHAPTER 35
Chapter Tutorial

Modern Chapter 26   **The Superpowers in the Modern Era**

IDENTIFYING TERMS Choose the term or name that correctly matches each definition.

_____ 1. headquarters of the U.S. military   **a.** Brezhnev Doctrine

_____ 2. British Labour Party leader   **b.** Pentagon

_____ 3. stated Soviet intervention policies   **c.** glasnost

_____ 4. openness   **d.** Maastricht Treaty

_____ 5. agreement creating the European Union   **e.** Tony Blair

UNDERSTANDING MAIN IDEAS

1. What did President George Bush mean by "new world order"?

_____

_____

2. Why did some European countries oppose entry into the European Union?

_____

_____

3. What were the intentions of perestroika and glasnost?

_____

_____

4. What events took place in the United States on September 11, 2001?

_____

_____

5. Why did the United States take military actions against the government of Afghanistan known as the Taliban?

_____

_____

Chapter 35 Tutorial, continued

REVIEWING THEMES

1. Economics In most cases, how do economic difficulties lead to political change?

_____

_____

2. Government How did the communist states suppress dissent?

_____

_____

3. Global Relations What changes to European relations were brought about by the Helsinki Accords?

_____

_____

THINKING CRITICALLY

1. Analyzing Information How did human rights affect U.S. policies toward China and the Soviet Union?

_____

_____

2. Identifying Cause and Effect How was the Soviet Union affected by perestroika and glasnost?

_____

_____

WRITING ABOUT HISTORY

Imagining Imagine you are a Russian citizen. Write a brief paragraph telling how your life might have changed under perestroika and glasnost.

_____

_____

_____

IDENTIFYING TERMS Choose the term or name that correctly matches each definition.

_b (p. 964)_ **1.** headquarters of the U.S. military   **a.** Brezhnev Doctrine

_e (p. 949)_ **2.** British Labour Party leader   **b.** Pentagon

_a (p. 956)_ **3.** stated Soviet intervention policies   **c.** glasnost

_c (p. 957)_ **4.** openness   **d.** Maastricht Treaty

_d (p. 955)_ **5.** agreement creating the European Union   **e.** Tony Blair

UNDERSTANDING MAIN IDEAS

1. What did President Bush mean by "new world order"?

Nations would work together to defend weaker countries. (p. 944)

2. Why did some European countries oppose entry into the European Union?

Some members of the EEC worried that the EU would undermine their sovereignty. (p. 955)

3. What were the intentions of perestroika and glasnost?

Gorbachev relaxed government control of the economy and eased restrictions on dissent. (p. 957)

4. What events took place in the United States on September 11, 2001?

Several hijacked passenger airplanes were purposefully crashed into the World Trade Center and the Pentagon. (p. 964)

5. Why did the United States take military actions against the government of Afghanistan known as the Taliban?

U.S. forces launched a series of powerful airstrikes against Afghan military targets because the Taliban had supported Osama bin Laden and his terrorist network called al Qaeda. (pp. 968–969)

REVIEWING THEMES

1. Economics In most cases, how do economic difficulties lead to political change?

People facing rising unemployment and inflation protest the policies of their government. Economic troubles often lead to political change. (p. 948–953)

2. Government How did the communist states suppress dissent?

They treated political opponents harshly, sometimes violently. (pp. 956–963)

3. Global Relations What changes to European relations were brought about by the Helsinki Accords?

They gave Europeans a new framework for economic and technological cooperation and provided a peaceful means for settling certain boundary disputes. They also called on all members to respect human rights. (pp. 953–954)

THINKING CRITICALLY

1. Analyzing Information How did human rights affect U.S. policies toward China and the Soviet Union?

The United States denounced Chinese human rights policies, and the United States protested the Soviet invasion of Afghanistan with the Carter Doctrine. (pp. 944–945)

2. Identifying Cause and Effect How was the Soviet Union affected by perestroika and glasnost?

Foreign relations improved; however, shortages of goods still existed although selection had improved. Opposition leaders organized a coup. (p. 957)

WRITING ABOUT HISTORY

Imagining Imagine you are a Russian citizen. Write a brief paragraph telling how your life might have changed under perestroika and glasnost.

Student responses will vary.

STUDY TIPS

1. Have students write a paragraph explaining the importance of national unity in the face of attack.

2. Have students research and make a chart outlining the conflicts in Afghanistan in the last 50 years.

CHAPTER 36

Modern Chapter 27

Chapter Tutorial

The Modern World

IDENTIFYING TERMS Choose the term or name that correctly matches each definition.

_____ **1.** form of art

_____ **2.** first person to orbit the earth

_____ **3.** making things smaller

_____ **4.** regulates the earth's temperature

_____ **5.** migration from countryside to city

a. Yury Gagarin

b. greenhouse effect

c. miniaturization

d. abstract expressionism

e. urbanization

UNDERSTANDING MAIN IDEAS

1. How did poetry and novels written in the years after 1945 reflect postwar society around the world?

_____

_____

2. What major advances in medical science have taken place since 1945?

_____

_____

3. What event increased public awareness of the dangers of pesticides?

_____

_____

4. What is the greatest challenge in addressing human rights?

_____

_____

5. What evidence exists that democracy spread in the late 1900s?

_____

_____

REVIEWING THEMES

1. Culture What direction did development in the arts and literature follow in the years after World War II?

_____

_____

2. Science, Technology, and Society How can technological change affect ideas and behavior?

_____

_____

3. Citizenship What challenges to well-being can people expect in the future?

_____

_____

THINKING CRITICALLY

1. Evaluating How might rapid population growth slow down other types of growth?

_____

_____

2. Drawing Inferences What might be some of the positive and negative results of genetic engineering?

_____

_____

WRITING ABOUT HISTORY

Persuading Write a brief paragraph explaining how the rights of children have changed in the last century.

_____

_____

_____

_____

_____

IDENTIFYING TERMS Choose the term or name that correctly matches each definition.

_d (p. 974)_ **1.** form of art

_a (p. 982)_ **2.** first person to orbit the earth

_c (p. 983)_ **3.** making things smaller

_b (p. 989)_ **4.** regulates the earth's temperature

_e (p. 988)_ **5.** migration from countryside to city

a. Yury Gagarin

b. greenhouse effect

c. miniaturization

d. abstract expressionism

e. urbanization

UNDERSTANDING MAIN IDEAS

1. How did poetry and novels written in the years after 1945 reflect postwar society around the world?

Many poets and novelists took a stand against the comfortable self-satisfaction they saw in the world around them. Some writers criticized postwar wealth and materialism; others emphasized continued racism, while still others provoked controversy in their writings. (p. 979)

2. What major advances in medical science have taken place since 1945?

Treatment of disease with antibiotics, polio vaccine, AIDS research and treatments, and discovery and mapping of the human genetic code. (pp. 986–987)

3. What event increased public awareness of the dangers of pesticides?

Publication of Silent Spring _by Rachel Carson in 1962. (p. 988)_

4. What is the greatest challenge in addressing human rights?

The concept of human rights does not have a single, universal meaning. Different cultures look at human rights in different ways. Some cultures place a greater importance on the interests of the community over the rights of the individual. (p. 992)

5. What evidence exists that democracy spread in the late 1900s?

The Soviet Union has rejected communism, and many authoritarian regimes have lost to democracy. (p. 992)

REVIEWING THEMES

1. Culture What direction did development in the arts and literature follow in the years after World War II?

There was more freedom of expression and fewer standards. (p. 974)

2. Science, Technology, and Society How can technological change affect ideas and behavior?

Ideas and information are transmitted quickly across social and cultural boundaries. (p. 985)

3. Citizenship What challenges to well-being can people expect in the future?

New ways to combat disease will bring greater feelings of safety; however, the effects of genetic engineering may pose troubling ethical questions. Pollution, overpopulation, and continued industrialization will also challenge the well-being of humans. (pp. 985–989)

THINKING CRITICALLY

1. Evaluating How might rapid population growth slow down other types of growth?

It will put further demands on limited resources. (p. 988)

2. Drawing Inferences What might be some of the positive and negative results of genetic engineering?

Students might say that medical gains will be positive; however, issues such as selective abortion and designer babies will create ethical dilemmas. (pp. 975–983)

WRITING ABOUT HISTORY

Persuading Write a brief paragraph explaining how the rights of children have changed in the last century.

Student responses will vary; however, they might mention child labor laws and compulsory schooling. (p. 993)

STUDY TIPS

1. Have students write a paragraph explaining the universal themes expressed through music, art, literature, dance, and architecture.

2. Ask students to diagram the development of the computer, charting the advances in society that have come about with increased computer use.

(EPILOGUE)

Chapter Tutorial

The Modern World

IDENTIFYING TERMS Choose the term or name that correctly matches each definition.

_____ 1. established power of Parliament over the ruler   **a.** capitalism

_____ 2. individuals control the factors of production   **b.** Bolsheviks

_____ 3. overthrew Kerensky government   **c.** Marshall Plan

_____ 4. European Recovery Plan   **d.** English Bill of Rights

_____ 5. racial separation   **e.** apartheid

UNDERSTANDING MAIN IDEAS

1. What is the British policy of mercantilism?

_____

_____

2. What were the terms of peace for Germany and the Allied powers as spelled out by the Treaty of Versailles?

_____

_____

3. What were the immediate results for China after the Tiananmen Square massacre in the spring of 1989?

_____

_____

4. What were some of the concerns in Russia when Boris Yeltsin's successor Vladimir Putin assumed power in Russia?

_____

_____

5. Why was it difficult for the United States to strike against terrorists outside the United States?

_____

_____

Epilogue Tutorial, continued

REVIEWING THEMES

1. Government Explain the differences between England's Tories and Whigs in the 1640s.

_____

_____

2. Economics How did the United States influence economic development in Latin America?

_____

_____

_____

3. Culture What were some of the major changes in art and literature in the late 1900s?

_____

_____

_____

THINKING CRITICALLY

1. Making Predictions What conflicts and debates might arise in the future in regard to cloning?

_____

_____

2. Supporting a Point of View In your opinion what was the greatest invention of the 1900s? Give at least two reasons to support your answer.

_____

_____

_____

WRITING ABOUT HISTORY

Persuading Pretend you are in Germany in 1989 and witness the fall of the Berlin Wall. Write a brief letter to family in the United States telling them of the exciting developments.

_____

_____

_____

_____

IDENTIFYING TERMS Choose the term or name that correctly matches each definition.

_d (p. 452)_ **1.** established power of Parliament over the ruler

_a (p. 454)_ **2.** individuals control the factors of production

_b (p. 459)_ **3.** overthrew Kerensky government

_c (p. 465)_ **4.** European Recovery Plan

_e (p. 472)_ **5.** racial separation

a. capitalism

b. Bolsheviks

c. Marshall Plan

d. English Bill of Rights

e. apartheid

UNDERSTANDING MAIN IDEAS

1. What is the British policy of mercantilism?

Held that the colonies existed for the economic benefit of the home country (p. 452)

2. What were the terms of peace for Germany and the Allied powers as spelled out by the Treaty of Versailles?

Germany was ordered to pay $33 billion in reparations. It also lost a large amount of land along its northern, western, and eastern borders, as well as its overseas colonies. Germany also had to agree not to fortify Rhineland. (p. 459)

3. What were the immediate results for China after the Tiananmen Square massacre in the spring of 1989?

In response to China's crackdown on demonstrators, many countries imposed economic sanctions. Tourism dwindled and the Chinese economy weakened. (p. 469)

4. What were some of the concerns in Russia when Boris Yeltsin's successor Vladimir Putin assumed power in Russia?

People feared Putin would suppress dissent and strengthen the central government at the expense of civil rights. (p. 475)

5. Why was it difficult for the United States to strike against terrorists outside the United States?

It would be difficult to identify the proper targets, as well as find and destroy them. (p. 483)

REVIEWING THEMES

1. Government Explain the differences between England's Tories and Whigs in the 1640s.

Tories usually supported the Anglican Church. As believers in a hereditary monarchy, however, they would be willing to accept a Roman Catholic king. The Whigs wanted a strong Parliament and opposed having a Catholic ruler. (p. 451)

2. Economics How did the United States influence economic development in Latin America?

Through the creation of trade alliances such as the North American Free Trade Agreement (NAFTA) (p. 467)

3. Culture What were some of the major changes in art and literature in the late 1900s?

Artists looked for new ways to work with ideas, images, and color. New materials and techniques were adopted in architecture and there was experimentation in the world of music and filmmaking. (p. 476)

THINKING CRITICALLY

1. Making Predictions What conflicts and debates might arise in the future in regard to cloning?

Students' responses might include ethical and religious questions, the right of the individual, and overpopulation (p. 477)

2. Supporting a Point of View In your opinion what was the greatest invention of the 1900s? Give at least two reasons to support your answer.

Student answers will vary, but should include a supporting statement.

WRITING ABOUT HISTORY

Persuading Pretend you are in Germany in 1989 and witness the fall of the Berlin Wall. Write a brief letter to family in the United States telling them of the exciting developments.

Student answers will vary.

STUDY TIPS

1. Ask students to write a paragraph describing the changes in human rights in Russia under perestroika and glasnost.

2. Have students create a time line of events of September 11, 2001.

PROLOGUE

Chapter Tutorial

The Ancient World

IDENTIFYING TERMS Choose the term or name that correctly matches each definition.

_____ **1.** spread of cultural aspects from place to place   **a.** caste system

_____ **2.** distinct social classes   **b.** direct democracy

_____ **3.** all citizens participate in making state decisions   **c.** adobe

_____ **4.** sun-dried brick   **d.** Augustus

_____ **5.** the revered one   **e.** cultural diffusion

UNDERSTANDING MAIN IDEAS

1. Where did the first civilizations develop?

_____

_____

2. What were the major accomplishments in science and medicine during the golden age in India?

_____

_____

3. What were the major accomplishments in mathematics, science, philosophy, and medicine during the golden age of Greece?

_____

_____

4. What were the main causes of the fall of the Roman Empire?

_____

_____

5. How did the spread of Islam in East Africa in the A.D. 700s influence trade?

_____

_____

_____

Prologue Tutorial, continued

REVIEWING THEMES

1. Government What was the danger of the Pax Romana system of government?

_____

_____

2. Geography Explain why Chinese civilization developed without outside influences.

_____

_____

3. Culture How did Greek culture spread during the period known as the golden age?

_____

_____

THINKING CRITICALLY

1. Contrasting Explain the differences between Daoism and Legalism.

_____

_____

2. Summarizing What were some of the main achievements of the first civilizations of the western Fertile Crescent?

_____

_____

WRITING ABOUT HISTORY

Persuading Write a brief paragraph explaining how the teachings of Jesus affected the Roman Empire.

_____

_____

_____

IDENTIFYING TERMS Choose the term or name that correctly matches each definition.

_e (p. 4)_ **1.** spread of cultural aspects from place to place

a. caste system

_a (p. 6)_ **2.** distinct social classes

b. direct democracy

_b (p. 11)_ **3.** all citizens participate in making state decisions

c. adobe

_c (p. 19)_ **4.** sun-dried brick

d. Augustus

_d (p. 14)_ **5.** the revered one

e. cultural diffusion

UNDERSTANDING MAIN IDEAS

1. Where did the first civilizations develop?

The first civilizations that we know of developed in or around four great river valleys: the Nile valley in Africa, the Tigris-Euphrates valley in Southwest Asia, the Indus valley in South Asia, and the Huang valley in East Asia. (p. 4)

2. What were the major accomplishments in mathematics, science, philosophy, and medicine during the golden age in India?

Indian mathematicians understood abstract numbers and negative numbers, astronomers understood the rotation of the earth on its axis, and Indian physicians invented the technique of inoculation, which is the procedure of immunizing people against disease. (p. 8)

3. What were the major accomplishments in mathematics, science, philosophy, and medicine during the golden age of Greece?

Greek thinkers tried to find logical explanations for natural events. Pythagoras wrote that everything could be explained through numbers and the relationship between them, and Hippocrates taught that disease came from natural causes and not as punishment from the gods. Greek philosophers focused on the mind. (pp. 12–13)

4. What were the main causes of the fall of the Roman Empire?

Civil war and invasions caused the fall. Within the span of 50 years no less than 18 men claimed the title of emperor. It cost a lot of money to defend the frontiers, and with the decline of expansion, income declined. Economic problems coupled with invasions from outsiders made life in the Roman Empire very difficult. (p. 16)

5. How did the spread of Islam in East Africa in the A.D. 700s influence trade?

By creating good conditions for trade (p. 18)

REVIEWING THEMES

1. Government What was the danger of the Pax Romana system of government?

The political system that Augustus and his successors created greatly reduced the traditional powers of the Roman Senate, the assemblies, and the magistrates. Political power was centralized in the hands of the emperor. As a result, there was always the danger that an emperor would abuse his vast powers. (p. 14)

2. Geography Explain why Chinese civilization developed without outside influences.

China was cut off from other civilizations by geographical features such as the Gobi and the towering mountains of central Asia. (p. 9)

3. Culture How did Greek culture spread during the period known as the golden age?

Greek culture spread through trade and colonization. (p. 12)

THINKING CRITICALLY

1. Contrasting Explain the differences between Daoism and Legalism.

Daoists believed that people should withdraw and think about the natural harmony of the world. The Legalists believed that people were basically selfish and untrustworthy and had to be controlled with harsh measures. (p. 10)

2. Summarizing What were some of the main achievements of the first civilizations of the western Fertile Crescent?

The Phoenicians developed the alphabet upon which our alphabet is patterned. The Lydians are remembered as the first people in history to use coined money, beginning in about 600 B.C. (p. 6)

WRITING ABOUT HISTORY

Persuading Write a brief paragraph explaining how the teachings of Jesus affected the Roman Empire.

Student answers will vary, but should include that Christianity's appeal was strengthened, in part, by increased violence and unrest that threatened the Roman Empire. (p. 15)

STUDY TIPS

1. Have students draw a graph outlining the fall of the Roman Empire, making sure to list the causes and effects.

2. Ask students to write a brief paragraph in which they pretend to be a Hopewell Indian explaining to a settler why the tribe built mounds.